Our Grandmothers, Ourselves

Reflections of Canadian Women

Edited by Gina Valle

Foreword by Joy Kogawa

Fitzhenry & Whiteside

First published in 1999 by Raincoast Books

Published in 2005 by Fitzhenry & Whiteside

Published in Canada by Fitzhenry & Whiteside, 195 Allstate Parkway, Markham, Ontario L3R 4T8

www.fitzhenry.ca   godwit@fitzhenry.ca

1   3   5   7   9   10   8   6   4   2

Library and Archives Canada Cataloguing in Publication

Our grandmothers, ourselves: reflections of Canadian
women / edited by Gina Valle; foreword by Joy Kogawa.

First published: Vancouver: Raincoast Books, 1999.
ISBN 1-55041-988-9

1. Grandmothers—Literary collections. 2. Grandparent and child—
Literary collections. 3. Canadian literature (English)—Women authors.
I. Valle, Gina, 1962-

PS8237.G73O97 2005   C810.8'035253   C2005-901135-1

Fitzhenry & Whiteside acknowledges with thanks the Canada Council for the Arts, the Government of Canada through the Book Publishing Industry Development Program (BPIDP), and the Ontario Arts Council for their support of our publishing program.

Special thanks to the following individuals for permission to reproduces their photographs: Nora Lusterio, Anna Lusterio and Rennie Lusterio, page 12; Vivian Hansen, page 22; Christine Bellini, page 30; Harriett Grant and Laniel Grant, page 41; Helen (Bajorek) MacDonald and Christine Bajorek, page 51; Natsuko Kokubu, page 60; Elpida Morfetas ans Sophia Morefetas, page 74; Nicola Lyle, page 85; Erika Willaert, page 94; Eva Tihanyi, page 103; Alanna F. Bondar and Arthur Bondar, page 110; Dimple Raja, page 118; Susan Evans Shaw and Deborah Dostal, page 125; Karen Diaz, page 133; Jo-Anne Berman, page 141; Gina Valle and Domenico Valle, page 149; Zeynep Varoglu, page 158.

Printed in Canada

TO MY PARENTS, WHOSE INFINITE, TRUSTING LOVE
HAS SHAPED THE WAY I VIEW THE WORLD.

TO MY GRANDMOTHER, WHO HAS LOVED ME
AS HER DAUGHTER.

– GV

Contents

Foreword

Grandmothers should be ruling the world. I say this without a hint of a joke. Grandmothers see the future in a way others do not. As the world of the flesh decays, the life of the spirit flowers. Grandmothers are a field of wildly blooming, exquisite and riotous flowers.

I know all this to be true because, having become a grandmother, I have felt an indescribably powerful force within – the love that surrounds a baby. Other grandmothers know about this. When we meet, we recognize the phenomenon. New grandmothers say in awe, "I never knew it would be like this. It's like being in love."

How blessed is the baby that knows a grandmother. Of course there are exceptions – every category has its aberrations. But as a species, grannies are uniquely loving, long-sighted – viscerally connected to past and future. In a cut-flower world, grandmothers connect. Their boundless hearts encompass the generations. And as the seedlight within them shines, their power moves on in the bright hearts of the babies they touch and love.

Blessed are the grandmothers for they secure the future. Blessed are their eyes for they see with love. Blessed are their hands, tireless in holding the babies of the world. Blessed are their feet, hastening to the baby's cry. Blessed are their bodies, given for birthing in the past, given to loving always. Blessed is the light in which they live and move and have their being. Blessed be grandmothers.

Blessed be.

JOY KOGAWA

7

Introduction

Our Grandmothers, Ourselves: Reflections of Canadian Women is a tribute to our grandmothers and the significant role they have played in shaping who we are. It celebrates the women who have bound us to our cultural and historical roots and honours the power of narrative to promote understanding among people of diverse backgrounds.

We, the contributors, are Canadian women raised in immigrant homes. To survive, we learned at an early age to tuck away our first language and culture as we scurried off to school each day. The effort to assimilate into the dominant culture left us little time or energy to examine our dual identity; many years of denial have kept us from sharing our experiences. In writing our stories, we establish a vital link with the past. Our voices speak with passion and dissonance as we redefine our identity in light of our grandmothers' experiences.

The grandmother-granddaughter relationship has undergone little examination in literature. In this collection, the portrayal of the grandmother is multidimensional – as woman, feminist, keeper of our first language and culture. These stories affirm that cultural heritage is manifested through language, food, storytelling, music, religion, holistic healing and symbols. Owing to our grandmothers' presence in our lives, these rich traditions will be preserved for yet another generation. Many of us were first awakened to issues of social justice, community, racism, self-esteem, equity, biculturalism, womanhood and family by our grandmothers.

IS GRANDMA A FEMINIST?

It is our hope that this cross-cultural collection will challenge the Western understanding of feminist ideology and encourage a more global perspective. Outside the Western world, feminism has historically been about protecting families and communities. Our grandmothers' survival depended on female networks; in this interdependency, these women were pioneers of feminist tradition.

Although our grandmothers, in breaking with traditional ground, function as feminist models, they rarely expressed ambivalence about their identity. At some point they were able to transgress the limitations of patriarchal societies. Through their unconditional love and strength, and through their power to inspire, they have undeniably influenced how we view ourselves as women.

GRANDMA TALKS FUNNY

Cultural heritage is inherent in language. As bicultural children, we inevitably face the loss of our first language in a land where English predominates, but our grandmothers keep the language of our ancestral lands alive within our homes.

Linguistic adaptation is a common immigrant experience. Often intergenerational ethnic families develop a language distinctly their own: there is a merging of two languages. Many of our grandmothers adapted to the English language by exchanging certain English words for those of their native tongues, and their mispronunciations and gestures formed the basis of a new linguistic expression.

IF GRANDMA TALKS FUNNY AND WE DON'T, THEN WHO THE HECK ARE WE?

Implicit in these stories is the dilemma of ethnic identity. Culture and language affect each person differently, and we are each faced with the rewards and pain of biculturalism. What we know of the world arises from our experience of that world; as immigrant children, we are bicultural individuals who have learned to view reality from multiple vantage points.

Within these intricate aspects of identity lies the universal notion of continuity. To know one's origin is to have a sense of belonging from which personal and social meaning is derived. Our grandmothers have bequeathed to us a value system that marks our heritage.

I REMEMBER THE STORIES GRANDMA
USED TO TELL US FROM THE OLD COUNTRY

Folktales and myths are powerful methods for teaching what is important in a culture, and the creative force of oral storytelling predominates in a number of these stories. Many of us come from cultures in which captivating tales are told rather than read. Our grandmothers have played a pivotal role in our family histories, and we have provided them with the opportunity to tell this history. Through their stories we vicariously experienced our grandmothers' adaptability and resilience in the face of hardship and have gained insight into their wisdom.

We hope this anthology will foster understanding of the multicultural character and ethnic diversity of our Canadian land. As we unravel the differences behind each of our stories, we come to discover the commonalties in our relationships with our babcias, obachaans, grannies, nonnas, yiayias and babas. It is our hope that *Our Grandmothers, Ourselves: Reflections of Canadian Women* will bring an increased awareness of the multiple perspectives through which reality may be viewed.

GINA VALLE

Passages

NORA LUSTERIO
ANNA LUSTERIO

1914. Corregidor, Philippines. Cecilia Cortez Solanoy was five years old, and it was nap time. Cecilia's mother's voice escaped from somewhere beneath the ceiling of the dense forest canopy, calling, *Halika na dito anak.* The foreign human pitch dispersed the birds in a noisy flurry; their sudden winged departure lifted a curtain of leaves and shook free some days' worth of collected rain. Cecilia listened and watched from the damp floor of the jungle. She was always listening and watching, her eyes like deep brown muddy waters trapped with secrets. A fluttering insect zigzagged in the warm air above her head; she longed to catch it. *Come up here now darling. Climb up here for sleep.* Cecilia heard clearly. A shiver of happiness and delicious fear ran through her because she had been hatching a plan all morning, a plan for this midday nap. She hurried toward her mother's voice, slapping the thick bamboo stilts at the base of the hut as she ran by, scattering the ants. As she climbed the ladder, she paused midway, suspended, bare feet hooked on the rung like limp fish; she was thinking. By the time she reached the final rung, her mother's broad back was turned, as Cecilia had hoped. Unseen, she grabbed a corner of the straw mat on which they slept and tugged once, swiftly and

11

In the Philippines, the Tagalog word for grandmother is lola. *But in our extended family, everyone called our grandmother* Nanay. Nanay *means mother. The style of the following story is patchwork to mimic the weaving of our grandmother's life with the lives of those who loved her as their matriarch.*

⌒ NORA LUSTERIO

Nanay's story, like her life, speaks for itself.

⌒ ANNA LUSTERIO

hard. A small triangle of rattan flooring lay exposed, with the open slat between two planks affording her a view of the dark underside of the hut. Cecilia stifled her glee and shifted her body to hide the dog-eared corner of the mat.

Her mother soon joined her, settling heavily in the oppressive heat, hugging her daughter to her. They lay in the room's shadows, tucked together, but not for long. Cecilia unfurled her arms from the comforting hollow of her mother's neck; she would need those arms. With her eyelids shut tight and the world gone all red and kind of spotty, Cecilia listened. Young green branches rubbed against the hut, producing an odd high squeak; this comical sound affected her like a tickle. She laughed.

A. Lusterio
3641, rue Ste-Famille, Apt. 14
Montreal, Quebec
Oct. 22, 1980

Mrs. Cecilia Cortez Solanoy
4 Varsity Avenue
Sault Ste. Marie, Ontario P6A 5T8

Dear Nanay,

I am very happy here at University and I really like my new apartment. Hope you are OK. Thank you for the prayer you sent to me. I hope it will help me do well on my exams. No, I do not have a boyfriend. I am studying too hard. How is your garden? I can't wait for Thanksgiving. I am taking the train on Friday. I want to taste the zucchini and green mustard that you have grown this year. Mom says you have been very busy harvesting and preparing the garden for winter. Hope you aren't working too hard. Say hi to Mom and Dad and everybody. I'll see you soon. I miss you very, very much.

Love always, A.

P.S. Please remember me in your prayers, especially for exams.

I smile as I type this letter, thinking of seeing my grandmother, Nanay, again and imagining her face as I recount all the adventures I have saved for her, all the new things I have seen and am learning about here in the big city of Montreal, 12 long hours away from home. I remember her advice to me on my last night in the Sault. We were smoking cigarettes in the living room: mine just two puffs old, hers smokeless and smouldering, with the lit end – I still don't know how – in her mouth. She removed her cigarette, spat out her mouthful of ash-blackened saliva and pronounced, "Nonette, you must beware op men. All dey want to do is puck you." At that moment, I became aware that my grandmother was more than "Nanay," the comforting, always-there person who had helped raise me and my three siblings. She knew about sex! She knew about men! She knew what "fuck" meant! She was an adult, a woman – a fascinating stranger. In my surprise and confusion, I said nothing, simply wished I had met this person sooner. I could have asked her so many things, in that risk-free and unabashed way one strikes up a conversation with a never-before-met yet comfortably familiar seatmate on a plane. She could have answered so many questions. I could have been better prepared for leaving home. Before I could speak, Nanay put her cigarette back in her mouth, folded her hands and began to contemplate her swollen feet, beached there on the coffee table. The stranger had gotten off the plane – and I'd neglected to get her address. But why fret? We would meet again. I was only 18. There would be plenty of time.

Above their heads, the long and graceful limb of a guava tree reached into the open window. Cecilia groped for its fruit, but her mother whispered, *Don't pick it, it's not ready. You must wait.* Well, Cecilia would wait. She was forever waiting and patient, for wasn't childhood endless! Agonizing minutes passed, minutes that seemed like hours before her mother's breathing fell to an even, audible rhythm. Cecilia opened one eye and stroked her mother's cheek. The gentle woman did not wake, and it was sweet relief for Cecilia to no longer have to contain herself. Squiggling onto her belly, she again pulled back the corner of the mat and fixed her eye through the narrow space between the floor's planks.

Her heart raced with a sudden, mad curiosity to know whether it was true, whether she was wrenched from play every day because of the mortal dangers of *aswang*, never had she seen these vampires that supposedly frightened their domestic animals away. Long had she suspected that at high noon the pig and chickens left the underside of the hut not out of fear, but in search of cooler shade. She would stay awake under the afternoon's thick blanket of heat with her watchful eye focused on the litter of feathers and sleeping chickens below while her mother slept, so still and so safe and so warm. And she would know.

Do not go to sleep with your hair wet, or when you wake up it will be all white. Dream of goldfish, it means you will be rich. If the letters of your name and the name of your fiancé add up to 25, your marriage will be happy. I knew of a boy, he died when a baseball hit him in his chest. Drink water after every bath – it will prevent nosebleeds.

Nanay's sweet tidbits of wisdom. Sprinkled liberally, generously, into my consciousness; tested suspiciously by me over the years in an attempt to . . . what? Tempt fate? See what would happen if . . . ?

"Anna, are you going to sleep now?"

"Yes, Nanay."

"Did you not have a shower?"

"Yes, Nanay." Mental smirk. Wait, does she notice my hair?

Disbelieving what she is seeing, her soft, dry fingers probe and grip my dripping ponytail. No words come; she continues with her crocheting. I go to bed feeling supreme, victorious, as if I had won something. My pillow is soaked. I truly feel shitty.

Oh, but the memory of an old woman was cruel. Its trapdoor blew open and shut on a whim. Cecilia tried to recollect more but could not. Then her senses returned, as they do after daydreams, one by one: sight, smell, sound. She heard the peculiar, insistent cries of Canada geese. She tipped up her chin to follow their flight. Fleeing from the torments of her grandchildren, the birds honked in an aggravated chorus of complaint.

They soared into the overcast sky above the choppy waters of Lake Superior, doubling back and finally ascending in twos and threes over the jagged treeline. She sat by the shore and poked holes in the sand with her cane. Two granddaughters ran by, scattering her thoughts, and Cecilia turned her head in an automatic inventory of the boys: there they stood, their sweater-clad figures perched like bright birds on a rocky promontory. They shouted and sang out across the open waters with challenge and daring in their voices. Cecilia, looking away, reflected mildly, *These children have strength.* She masked her grin of approval behind the collar of her coat.

With Nanay, open-ended questions were the most effective: "Nanay, what were you like when you were young?"

"Oh, I was very bold. When I was young, my father bought me new shoes. I liked nice clothes, nice shoes. Many times, the boys would come to visit me, to woo me. And you know what I did? I would show them the shoes on my feet." She held her slippered feet up in front of her, recalling what she had said: *"'Do you see these shoes? They cost more than your salary!' And I would laugh. Oh, I was very bold when I was young. . . .*

"When I became a widow, I lived in our house alone with your mother and our servant, Lucas. We were still rich because your grandfather had made much money with his selling, and we still had some left. One day, a man came. From our village. He wanted to marry me! So you know what I did? I showed my machete to him and shook it and shouted, 'Go away from here! I don't want you!' After that, he went away. He was ugly. . . .

"One time your grandfather and I were walking in the street and I saw him looking at a woman. So I boxed his ears and said, 'Hey! What are you looking at?' . . .

"During the war, there was no food. We had to hide in the forest, from the Japanese. For food, Lucas and I would go into the fields to look for a cow. Then we would kill it and take the meat for trading. If we had been caught, we would have been shot."

When Cecilia looked again to the late-afternoon sky, she spied, buried deep in its stormy promise, the hint of an omen. Sensing its darkness, she tried to shake herself free of the message it wanted to send her. She kept her eyes downcast but swift clouds threw strange patches of shadow upon the ground before her, bidding her to take heed. So she listened. It was not long before a strange whisper found an echo in the hollow of her ear, and she concentrated, straining to hear.

This was what she heard – it was a sentence that had issued before from the lips of her beloved Canadian-born grandchildren: *I am the first generation.* She had been puzzled, when she first heard it. What did it mean? In any case she'd forgotten it. Now she mouthed it back to the wind that sounded it out for her a second time: *I am the first generation.* And she was greatly surprised when a feeling of terrible loss blew forcefully into her heart.

Ah, loss. So it was that. Loss followed her everywhere. The years of the Second World War, for example, had been hard. She thought on these years briefly, holding out her long fingers in the counting: she'd lost a baby toe to gangrene, her baby girl to a burst appendix, her husband to shrapnel, their fortune to thieves, her cow and chickens to Japanese soldiers and her female neighbours to American husbands. And now – so. Even her losses were thrown to the winds and forgotten. Even the losses were stolen from the children for whom she had suffered them. *I am the first and the only generation.* Was that it, truly? Expressionless, she watched the horizon darken in its own torment.

Alma Solanoy Lusterio
34 Roselawn, Apt. 21
Toronto, Ontario
June 25, 1963

Dear Nanay: I am pregnant. Your first Canadian grandchild is due in September. . . .

I imagine Nanay didn't need to read more than that to decide to come to Canada and help her only daughter. Her Alma, her soul, the one who'd gone to university, become a nurse and was now living so far away. Working, and now with a child on the way. It would be hard. The need was unuttered but undeniable, like the invisible, insistent pull of an ocean tide. Who knows what Nanay felt as she booked a passage from her island of bamboo and heat to the continent of concrete and snow? There are no pictures of her voyage, only a rare recounting of how, arriving at a U.S. airport with little money and less English, she managed to make the connecting flight out of the confusion and find her way to her daughter. And to us, her first-generation Canadian grandchildren.

Goodbye, Cecilia. Hello, Nanay.

Cecilia could not protect her grandchildren from fate; this she knew. Yet was this their fate? To be *first generation?* The idea careened madly in her head, wanting badly to right itself. Why come to a new country to suffer erasure? Why lose what was rightfully theirs, the hard-won lessons of her life, to forgetfulness? This thing of their history, this thing called their past. It belonged to the family, ran thick in their blood. It was a weight, it was a rootedness – air stinging the nostrils, half-choked in heavy rains, the forest alive in its nervous and chattering awareness of distant typhoons. This was all she knew and all she could give them. But it was not unheard of for children to reject their inheritance.

Her thoughts tugged deep furrows into her brow. She rose to occupy herself with the gathering of pebbles, cool and smooth and lighter in hue when rubbed dry. Yet even as she bent to choose this stone and that one, attempting to distract herself, her trouble persisted. Would even the languages be lost to them? She glanced around, and the young one was nearest. Cecilia called out to her, "*Halika na anak.* Come here. Let me comb your hair, tell you a story." But the child, her interest snagged on a log, pretended not to hear.

In her own life, a so-be-it acceptance of events as they happened was typical of Nanay and covered everything from money to marriage.

"During the war, it was very hard. Our neighbour's son, Amado, would bring us sugar or coffee. Every day, he walked along the beach, looking for these things – things to eat, things to sell. Many times, he found them washed up on the shore, in boxes; sometimes, he got them from the American military base. One evening he came to the house, bringing rice, so my father invited him to play dominoes with us. Every day after that, he would come, after supper, to play dominoes. Many months passed, and one night, my father got up from the game early; he was very tired and went to bed. Amado and I continued playing, playing. Then he gave me a piece of paper, folded many times so that it was very small. It said: 'I love you.' I was happy but I did not show it. I hid the note in my pocket, saying nothing. I was afraid my father would see it. When our game was finished, Amado left to go home, as usual. When he reached the bottom of the veranda stairs, I saw that he'd forgotten his hat. I ran after him calling out, 'Hey! Your hat!' And you know? When I gave it to him, he grasped my hand, pulled me to him and kissed me!" She laughs, her eyes crinkling up at the memory of surprise and joy, the back of her hand held up to her laughing mouth as if re-enacting the wiping away of the kiss. "My mother saw us kissing there, at the bottom of the stairs. She was very mad. Oh, very mad. She said, 'Now you must be married.' And so, we were married. He was a very kind man, your grandfather. And oh, so handsome. I loved him, too."

Wed at 14, widowed at 31. Yet, her love for her husband, like her wisdom, was ageless.

When we received the call that Nanay was ill, that it was near the end, my husband and I booked the earliest flight to the Sault. In the rented car, racing to the hospital, I cried as Eric Clapton's "Would You Know My Name?" played on the radio. I remember thinking how grey, how cold my hometown seemed. It is oddly embarrassing to admit that details like these actually occurred and are still remembered. After this, my memory allows replays of only painful, incomplete scenes: the sight of my husband sobbing against the wall of Nanay's hospital room; the drawn and terrified faces of my siblings who'd gathered from across the country, remembering that an earlier promised visit to see her had fallen through, thinking that none of us ever should have left her in the first place. It is like a bad movie, complete with clichés. You want to stop watching, but you can't.

On the last morning of her life, Cecilia's breathing was too laboured for her to pray. There was water in her lungs and a gurgle in her chest when her great-grandchild lay his ear there. After days and days of waiting for relief, her movements grew frantic and needy – arms reaching up and up, as if she were surfacing, as if she had been trying for hours to surface. Death looked like a slow drowning, from where we stood on the shore.

But I remember her hair poured out evenly onto the pillow, like the streaks behind a child's drawing of a star.

In my house is a rattan trunk full of runners and doilies, all crocheted by Nanay; all bearing traces of her familiar, comforting scent. They assault the eye with their riotous, dizzying patterns and unpredictable colour combinations. Some lie flat; most refuse to. Those made most recently are askew and asymmetrical, their untamed shapes freed by the imps of increasing blindness and memory loss. All are priceless to me.

I keep them preserved, separately, in small plastic bags. Every so often, when I'm feeling particularly brave, I'll choose one, open the bag and inhale.

Women of Letters

STORIES BREATHED TO ME BY MY MOTHER

VIVIAN HANSEN

It begins with the kale. Odd, leafy vegetable growing in my yard. I can't find a recipe for either plucking or cooking this bush until I find yours. The instructions are written in Danish, spidery broken lines of your peasant-farmwife words smudged upon the page.

No one in Canada knows what to do with kale.

I stand up in my yard to look at the deep-green bush, fingers frost frozen from the kale biting my hand, and am suddenly pleased with my secret: how to make *grønlångkol*. How did I learn this secret when I could not hear your voice, watch you cook, or smell the juices of your green stew? I had only your letters, and the stories breathed into me by my mother, who resuscitated me when my life became too antiseptically Canadian, my language too pure, my purse too pliant.

Mom saved the letters. The ones from you and Far Mor (Father's Mother). They are the threads that hold the needlepoint picture together, the portrait of immigration, the text[ile] of our life in this cold strange

I am a product of an age in Canadian history that lived in denial of its ethnicity. Researching my grandmothers' texts gave me permission, and a sense of pride in being "other." In writing, I came to realize the toll immigration has taken on our lives as first-generation Canadians.

— VIVIAN HANSEN

place called Canada. Now, reading them over, I can smell the pain of your distance, the agony of missing those you loved, like the smell of *grønkol* steaming from the smoked pork roast. The letters still come out strong, steeped in time and memory. The first one is about Olemor's (Great-grandmother's) death:

> October 6, 1957: Wednesday morning when I came to see them, grandma was very weak, and could not eat herself. I could tell from her eyes that things were bad. Around noon she had wanted to go to the toilet . . . but when she came to the kitchen door, she collapsed, probably from a heart attack . . . Grandpa saw this and cannot get over it; he cannot forget the sight of it.

This letter arrived a year and two months after my parents and two brothers immigrated to Calgary from rural Denmark. They knew no English when they arrived. My mother's only memories of this muteness were later expressed with the words, "It was bad, very bad." The next five years would be a struggle to lose their past and to master the new language of survival: English.

Caught up in that struggle, I learned to leave behind my m[other] tongue, the Danish that permitted primal feelings. So long was I caught up in learning English – its nuances, fears, hatreds and foolish mannerisms – that I nearly forgot you. English is the language of break-from-my-grandmothers, the language of utility. It has no heat in its cold roominess.

An old crocheted throw rests on my couch. It is your blanket, worked in green, yellow and black; a fabric now broken with years of use. When did you send it to us, and when did I think your text[ile] important enough to stitch together again? Perhaps when I translated your form, your letters.

> October 31, 1958: Dear Everybody: Thanks a lot for the beautiful picture of Vivian. Is she ever a beautiful little girl. We all sat around the table and looked at that picture. . . .

This is affirmation. I belonged to a people who lived across an ocean; people who spoke no English, whose language had room to enfold me. People who loved and missed my mother terribly. People who did not abuse or throw rocks at us because we were poor, uneducated, displaced persons. From time to time, my father's mother would write to her son:

> February 5, 1960: Dear Everybody: I want to wish you happiness and God's blessing on your birthday, Eduard. You are 40 years old now and I cannot understand that you, my oldest son, is now 40 years. How time goes and you are already that old. That is hard to understand. I would like to have been with you when you are celebrating your birthday, but obviously that cannot be done since you are so far away. . . .

The agony of distance eludes the stitch. The needlepoint pattern incomplete, we waited for another letter, temporarily unaware that we were actively stitching our own bland colours into the background.

My mother had to breathe life into these words, make sounds from the foreign symbols. Were it not for her, I would never have had these links to either of you. Bedstemor, she tells me of how she menstruated for a year before you discovered her blood. Shamed, fearful, she hid the signs of her budding womanhood from you. Grandfather, furious with you for neglecting your duty to your daughter. Mother, terrified that she was dying. She could not tell you, afraid of your fanaticism. This part of you, the part that caused my mother to shudder with frightened anticipation of your next letter:

> I pray that God in his mercy would send a big awakening out over the whole world so that we his people could get new power to follow him the last of the way that we have gone and that many, many people would be saved and become Jesus' children before it's too late. . . .

This piece is strangely detached from your life in the Viking longhouse, as though you searched for something that would complement your art, your intelligence, or perhaps something to forgive these two talents. I will never know, for my mother cannot breathe this part of you; she fears your voice still. I have come to realize that I knew only a mother who needed, in turn, to be mothered. She did not get this gentle knowing from you. I had to mother my own mother, she who was terrified of you. Minus the moan of "mmmm," we could only make the best of what was left: "other."

Mom speaks of the time she wrote a story for a magazine. The story was published, and she won a small bit of money. She did not tell you. When you found out, she heard only the lecture about how she should have tended to her chores instead of the "evil lies in writing."

What about your letters, Bedstemor? Were they evil? Or was writing the excuse you needed for communicating with your wayward daughter? Did you equate the letters with your *håndarbejde* (handiwork), crocheting the words to fashion a colourful piece of art?

Sometimes I stroke the crocheted tablecloth, the little-girl-lace-collars-with-mother-of-pearl-buttons, a blanket, a small rug. *Håndarbejde*. The stitches I must repair and string together again, the letters I must read in Danish. These items of *håndarbejde* are all I have left of you.

My mother, your daughter, is afraid even now of that handiwork. But she excuses your ferocity: "Bedstemor lived a hard life. She was sent out as a milkmaid when she was eight years old. Woke at 4:00 A.M. to milk the cows, then went to school at 8:00. She would lay her head down on the desk so tired that the teachers let her sleep."

When you awoke, you learned your letters.

No time for you to learn of love, your own mother unmentioned. Mother-hood in my family is disjointed, at best. A long legacy of disunity, confusion, but you pricked us with the pins of what kept your life intact:

Sunday, 19 June 1960: Today is a very cold day, but we still have to go and work in the field. If we don't, nothing is growing. This is not Søster's (mother's sister) big thing. She doesn't really like to work in the field, but she has to help. That's a farmer's way. You have to work to get the harvest and Søster doesn't seem to understand that.

Work. It is all you know. And when you allow yourself to think too much, holes are revealed and you must place the patchwork of religion over the gaps.

My brother, Thorkild, left our family for a year to go to Minnesota. An angry young man, he tired of the stigma of being an immigrant in Canada. He wearied also of the burdens he bore as the oldest son. Bedstemor nearly despaired of him:

> How does it go with Thorkild? Is he going back to the States again? Yes, I guess you can understand we are nosy to hear what he is doing and what his plans are for the future. Believe me, lille [little] Thorkild, we would like to follow up on what you are doing. We would like to know what you are thinking and we want you to know that we are praying for you every day. It's a long time since we have heard from him. I'm afraid he's going to forget the Danish language. Now he is in a strange country, he has no chance to hear Danish anymore.

You believed that only the sound of prayer could blow across the ocean to touch the ones you loved. And Far Mor? Five years after my family's immigration, her letters are agonizing in their loneliness, as though the finality of the break had suddenly become real to her:

> 1961: A blessed Christmas, my dear children, and thanks for putting up with me while I was in Canada last summer. I remember you very well, little Vivian. You were so good to me. Thanks for all the times you sat down and talked to me and kept me company. You were so little and I was just an old far mor.

I have memories of these grandmothers. This Far Mor, the one who argued with my mother about trivial things. I distracted her in order to keep peace in the family.

Memories. Snapshots in the mind. My mother's mother, tentative in her approaches to me when we visited Denmark in 1967. She was uncertain if I could function in the Danish language. It would have hurt her too much to be unable to speak to her granddaughter. I carry the names of both grandmothers: Maria and Anna = Marianna. The girl stitched together by her grandmothers.

Far Mor grew lonely and desperate, her grief at her separation from us pitiable:

> 1966: Dear children: Now we are again into a New Year. I got your letter December 23, just in time for Christmas. It is so good if you can take time to write to me. Sometimes I think I'm not worth it anymore. I can do nothing for you and your family and I would so much like to. My home is open to you all if you would take a holiday and come and visit me. I can still cook and bake the way you like it. In that way, I do not feel old. Next month is my 75th birthday.
> *(Maria died July 10, 1967)*

My maternal grandmother spent her last days in a nursing home, where she seems to have been content:

> When I was home, I always missed Far (father). I believe it is God that has guided me to live here, and that is why I am content with the knowledge that God is with me, in whatever I believe and whatever happens. This evening we are having a craft time, but I cannot see too well with the evening light, so I will stay in my room. This morning, another lady and I went for a walk for a couple of hours. Believe me, we were good and ready for dinner and then a little rest. Now look, what a long letter I have put

together. I almost thought I couldn't write anymore.

(Anna died December 28, 1975)

I stroke the crocheted throw and the lace collars you sent me when I was too small to know you. No longer usable, they are works of art – stitchery of stubborn survival, my only mementoes of you.

November 1994: Women's Studies 405 lecture; University of Calgary. Topic of Discussion: Betty Freidan, *The Feminine Mystique* (1963). Whose mother read this book? What did she say about it? How did this book contribute to your understanding of feminism? Your mother's?

Each woman responds in turn. Some identify with the "mystique." Theoretics. Personal Herstory. My turn arrives. I state haltingly that my mother did not read *The Feminine Mystique,* for she could barely read English. She could read the newspaper, perhaps, and some fundamental English text, but she read mostly my grandmothers' letters.

The classroom is quiet. The professor stares. I have once again declared my lower-class status, have differentiated between them and *me.* No one here is Immigrant. My feeling of uncertainty is familiar. In 38 years, I have never identified with Canadian women. I continue to be uncertain of my place in this society. But now, right now, I refuse to let the moment pass. I have power. "I can read," I announce, "my grandmothers' letters in Danish."

Who cares? Probably no one. But second-wave feminism is too polite to shut me down, even as it is too proper to welcome me.

June 1995: A staged walk. Convocation at the University of Calgary. Declaration: Vivian Marianna Hansen. Bachelor of Arts in English. I have mastered this foreign tongue at last. My root name an accretion of my two grandmothers, honoured in academia.

November 1995: My hands red with cold, I pluck the last of the kale. It is the only green vegetable that must not be picked until after a killing frost – the frost that takes the bitterness out of the leaves. I read your recipe, in Danish:

Gronkale must be cooked with smoked meat: a ham or pork

roast. Take ⁶ cup milk, 100 grams of butter, and warm in the casserole until butter is melted in milk. Chop *grønkol,* about 3 or 4 cups, and add to the milk and butter mixture, stirring often so it won't burn. Mix with mashed potatoes.

Writing about my grandmother was something I have wanted to do for years, but I was unable to express the love and the loss I felt. While I was researching stories about Nonna with my relatives, I gained a lot of insight from my Aunt Andea, who opened herself up to me. I therefore dedicate this story to her.

— CHRISTINE BELLINI

Memories of Maria

CHRISTINE BELLINI

My family and I stood around the hospital bed staring at my Nonna Bellini. She appeared so shrunken and distorted, only a semblance of the robust farm woman who once worked the fields and arm-wrestled with her sons. She had just had her third stroke and was in a coma. My brother leaned over the bed and gently took her hand. "Nonna," he whispered, "it's Paul." He turned to us in shock. "She just squeezed my hand – " I noticed both my uncles turn away with tears in their eyes. I felt my chest tighten and wondered how much more suffering this woman was to endure. Nonna had been battling Alzheimer's for years, and even though her will to live had diminished after my grandfather passed away, her body refused to die.

Holding Nonna's hand was the last contact we would have with her. We left the hospital and flew back to Toronto that day, only to discover that she had died as our plane was landing. Back in Northern Ontario 24 hours later, I stood over the body of my grandmother and thought that, finally, she was at peace. Many of her friends and relatives came to pay their respects, and as I stared at Nonna I knew I would feel her loss for years to come.

Twelve years afterwards, the legacy of Maria Bellini lives on through my brother and I. We take great pride in telling stories about her to our friends. Even though there are countless Bellini anecdotes, they all seem to convey the same message over and over again: that Maria Bellini was, and still is, a source of inspiration to us. Her robust personality and good nature allowed us to put our trust in her. Her unconditional love of her grandchildren was extremely special and rare. No matter what antics Paul and I were up to, whether drawing pictures under her kitchen table or rummaging through the cupboards for cookies, we knew that Nonna Bellini would never be angry with us.

The following stories are not just amusing and dramatic, but also express the influence my grandmother had on my life. She taught me that self-respect and honesty are two of the most important qualities to live by. Her strength runs through my blood, and through the blood of all of my relatives who, in some way, were touched by Nonna's love.

NONNA LIVED ON A FARM NEXT TO THE DRIVE-IN

My father grew up on a big farm in Northern Ontario that housed 13 people – my grandfather's family as well as his brother Mario's family. The farm was run by my grandmother and her sister-in-law Julia, who spent their days cooking, cleaning and maintaining order. Nine children lived on the farm, all of whom had to walk 10 miles every day to attend the public school in town. The long walk was always a source of great frustration to my father and his siblings, who enjoyed school but felt that their poverty and isolation limited their power to attend. My grandmother persuaded her children to attend school because she herself regretted her inability to pursue a career in nursing while growing up in Italy. As immigrants, my grandparents often felt shame over their lack of command of the English language, and wanted to make certain that their children would not carry the same burden.

In retrospect, my family views the years spent on the farm as harsh. They concentrated on surviving Canadian winters, feeding everyone, fighting off illnesses and coping with extreme isolation. Once all nine children were grown, my grandfather and his brother sold the farm and both moved to town. My grandfather bought a white-and-pink house on Kirby Avenue, and I spent a great deal of my childhood there. It was only one block away from my house, and I made many trips up and down the laneway that connected our two homes. This house was remarkable in one respect: the basement was divided between the first floor, where my grandparents lived, and an upstairs apartment. It was possible to open a glass door and enter the tenant's section of the basement. My brother and I would sneak into their section and pretend to be burglars. The basement also had a built-in winepress, a root cellar containing large tins of tomatoes and ceramic pots filled with sausages in oil, and a big table on which my grandmother would make pasta. It was a well lived-in home, unlike those of many Italian immigrants who at that time kept their couches and lamps wrapped in cellophane and confined themselves to a recreation room and basement kitchen. Nonna's home was distinct in that we were granted the run of the entire house. One of my favourite games was "elevator ride": I would hide inside a tall kitchen cupboard, close the door and yell, "Going up!" There was also an extremely tiny bedroom that we referred to as "the dungeon," in which Paul and I were allowed to jump all over the bed and play with religious paraphernalia.

I knew the farm only through black-and-white photographs and through our Saturday-night ritual of going to the drive-in close to where the farm had been. As we pulled up to the booth, our car stuffed with toys and pillows, my father would point to a vast field and tell us that that was where he'd grown up. I would stare into the blackness and ask the same question every time: "Did you watch movies from your bedroom window?" As a child, I could not grasp the hardships my father's family had endured, nor did I have the insight to recognize that my family's working-class ethic originated from the Bellini farm.

One morning my mother, Rena, was returning home from visiting her mother. As she opened the door to our house, a mouse ran across the kitchen floor. Rena screamed, grabbed the phone and called Nonna Bellini. "Come right over, there's a mouse in my house and I am not getting off the kitchen table until you get here." Nonna calmly replied, "Okay, I come over and *keeel.*" Rena, six months pregnant with me, stood patiently on the kitchen table, waiting for her mother-in-law to rescue her. Maria grabbed her broom and walked down the laneway with a mission in mind. She arrived, found the mouse and killed it. However, she gave my mother a warning: "Where there's one, there is many." Later on her words rang true, as our house was infested with mice. The story of Nonna saving my pregnant mother from a tiny mouse was always told with great comic zeal; however, we all knew that Maria could be counted on in times of crisis. The message conveyed time and time again was that Maria was not only competent during crises, she was compassionate as well. She did not mock or trivialize my mother's fear of mice, but handled the situation with her usual practicality.

NONNA KILLED CHICKENS WITH
DULL SCISSORS IN HER BASEMENT

As a child I remember the burlap bag moving and squawking on the floor of Nonna's basement. I stared at it in fear. They were *live* chickens. They could attack with their sharp beaks and claws, and were frantic, almost aware they were about to die. Nonna would pull one out of the bag and hold its neck over the sink, and with a dull pair of scissors she would cut its throat open and bleed it to death over cold running water. Later, she would hold the severed claw of the chicken in front of my brother's face and pull on its tendons. As the claw opened and shut, Paul would stare at her with a blank expression, but he was secretly repulsed. I thought it was great. I was not trying to grasp the meaning of life or death; I was wondering why my nonna was the only person I knew who did this. A few years ago I was surprised to hear another young Italian woman describe the same event taking place in her family. It was then I realized that killing chickens was a working-class ritual performed out of necessity to feed one's family.

Afterwards, Nonna would make chicken soup and drop dozens of yolks into the soup. They would burst in my mouth, and I thought, "How delicious and exciting. What if I bit into a baby chicken?" Our friends were always quick to ask, "What about the cholesterol in eating dozens of yolks?", but we never thought of cholesterol. We concentrated on the fact that Nonna was an incredible cook. Feeding her family was one of the ways she showed her love. It was Nonna who made all the classic meals that are inherent in our culture. On Sunday nights the family would meet at her house and settle down to bowls of strachetelle, plates of pasta, veal cutlets and roast potatoes saturated in lard. My mother learned to replicate many of these meals, and today when I go home and have a bowl of minestrone Maria style, the memories of her kitchen and our gatherings come back to me.

Gathering food from the earth included other activities for my family, such as maintaining large vegetable gardens. Nonna's garden consumed her entire yard, and I used to sit and hide in the pea patch, playing with bugs and eating dirty – but fresh – vegetables. My grandfather silently kept an eye on me as I sat on the cool earth, content with my pastoral surroundings.

Another form of gathering took place on Saturday mornings in the summer. We would drive out to the bush to pick blueberries, mushrooms or dandelions, our bodies sprayed with insect repellent and any exposed skin covered with clothing. I loved the adventure of romping through the bush. Paul did not, and he would lock himself in the car sulking with a *Mad Magazine*. Today, in urban settings, we have lost much of the ritual of gathering and hunting. New Age culture has attempted to revive many of these rituals, but these attempts, albeit token, are glorified versions of what was once a means of survival. For Maria Bellini, there was nothing romantic about picking dandelions in the bush. Rather, it was a practical and penniless way she could feed her family when money was scarce.

NONNA ATE RAW PORK
WHILE MAKING SAUSAGE

We would often spend Saturday nights at Nonna's house as she and her sons made sausage: a combination of raw pork, garlic and sausage casings soaked in wine. I would watch as my dad and his brother Victor took turns cranking the wheel of the stainless-steel sausage maker. Every once in a while Nonna would grab a handful of raw pork and eat it. My mother would always say the same thing: "Ma, you're going to get sick." "*Bullashit*," she would reply, and would keep on eating copious amounts of raw pork. I would stare at her in awe, admiring her defiance. Nonna ignored everybody's warnings that raw pork could give you worms and she refused to live in fear of what might happen. If I ate raw pork I probably would have puked, but seeing Nonna do this and never even seem ill invested her with godlike qualities.

What I liked most was Nonna's opposition in the face of group pressure, for there were many times I heard my grandmother stubbornly say "*bullashit*" to her family. Maria did not care what people said, but rather did whatever she thought was in her best interest. Maria fought the oppressors that tried to control her: the Catholic church, her family, the insular Italian community and small-town mentality. It took great strength to maintain any sense of autonomy in this environment. Witnessing my grandmother's incredibly strong will inspired me to fight back too.

NONNA HAD A MUSTACHE

Growing up in a western world that says blond is beautiful left me thinking that I was ugly. I was fat, hairy, short and dark. I wore long-sleeved shirts all summer to hide my hairy arms and secretly wished my round belly were really a pillow I could remove. Nonna Bellini had a mustache and refused to shave it off. Her family would often tell her to shave, to make her look more ladylike or less disturbing I assume, but she wouldn't do it. Nonna believed in looking straight into a person's face when talking, and I remember as a child her round face smiling directly at me. This was profoundly different from many other Italians, who, out of shame or feelings of inferiority, looked either down or away when speaking to others. Nonna's face was beautiful even as an old woman, and I would look at pictures of her when she was young, and think, "Now *that's* sexy."

Nonna did not believe in dieting, but rather in healthy living. She rarely drank, walked daily, and believed her body did not belong to anybody else but herself. Wife assault was well-known but silenced in the Italian community; however, my grandmother often told Nonno Bellini that if he ever beat her, she would beat him back. She could probably have made good on this threat as she was more than two hundred pounds of muscle, and my grandfather was small by comparison. She lectured her children on how wife assault was an attack on a woman's dignity. It was from Nonna that I developed my sense of self-respect and my concept of sensuality and sexuality. Maria was big, round and tactile. You could feel her body alive when you hugged her. You could see the strength in her arms when she arm-wrestled with her sons. You could see her sensuality when she wore dresses and showed off her legs. She was both profoundly masculine and profoundly feminine.

WE ALL STARED IN SHOCK AS NONNA SAID "FUCKA YOU" TO HER PURSE

My grandparents seemed to have a language of their own, a mix of English, Italian and slang. Italian mentality clashed with North American culture as Maria invented words such as "jongy," "basterdjay" and "feex." "Jongy" was Maria's interpretation of the word "junk" combined with the meaning of the word "trinket." Being a practical woman, Maria was not fond of knick-knacks, and whenever one was given to her as a gift, she referred to it as a "jongy." North American society often ridicules ethnic mispronunciation of English words and phrases, and Paul and I are no different. We would mimic my grandmother's accent to her face, but she was never insulted. She was aware of her mispronunciations. More important to her was her ability to express herself, no matter how obscure the words were to others.

One day Nonna, having dropped her purse on the floor, blurted out, "Fucka you." We all stared in shock. Nonna had said the "F word." Even though we all swore in our house, the "F word" was the limit. The night before, our local television channel had aired an uncensored version of the movie *Joe*. Obviously, Maria, along with everyone else in town, had watched the movie. The only difference was, everyone else watched it to hear "Fuck you," whereas Maria had no idea what that meant. My father, slightly exasperated, turned to his mother, and in Italian tried to explain to her the meaning of "Fuck you." It was one of those moments of humiliation immigrants often endure when they have unwittingly crossed a cultural barrier. Nonna never said "Fuck you" again, but she did pepper her dialogue with such great Italian profanities as *"merde."*

NONNA GOT ALZHEIMER'S

There is one special video that Paul and I have of Nonna at Christmas just prior to the onset of her illness. I was in my second year of university, and Paul and I had just discovered the joy of video. We arrived at Nonna's, and she was hacking away at a pork bone with a butcher knife and a hammer, preparing for tomorrow's meal with us. "Sonamabeech," she cursed, as the bone slipped from her mighty grip. Paul and I thought this very funny, but what we did not realize was that Nonna was extremely depressed. After my grandfather died, Nonna's will to live diminished and it became clear that she no longer felt needed by her family. All her grandchildren had grown up and moved away, and the meals that had meant so much to us faded into the past. For more than 60 years she had had a harmonious marriage with my grandfather; now, alone and isolated in Northern Ontario,

Nonna felt she had little joy left in her life. She did not want to burden her children, but for a woman who had lived most of her life surrounded by a large family who needed her, the reality of being alone morning and night – and of cooking and eating alone – was simply too much for her to take.

Two years later my parents informed me that Nonna had been brought to the hospital. She had suffered some kind of *breakdown*. Nonna remained there for a year, undiagnosed and left to rot. When I came home from university I would go visit her. As a granddaughter, there was nothing I could do for her, and my sense of powerlessness pained me. She would swear at the nurses and lash out at them, and at one point my father found her tied to the bed. Apparently she had hit a nurse with her cane and had been declared dangerous. Her treatment at the hospital was horrific. The hospital staff was not the least bit sensitive to her ethnicity or to her illness, and they both feared and despised this incredibly strong old woman. How could they make sense of her tears and yelling, since she had completely reverted to speaking Italian? My grandmother refused to eat hospital food. Despite her illness, she still had her standards. Every day my mother would make an Italian meal and bring it to her to eat so she would remain strong. Nonna appreciated the gesture of being fed by my mother, and as her mind deteriorated, she called my mother "Mama."

One of my last memories of my grandmother is of the time I went to visit her in the retirement home. She had been put in a wing especially for Alzheimer's patients, which had many security features to prevent patients from wandering off or harming themselves. It was summer, and I found her in the sealed-in backyard with other Alzheimer's patients, who were busy talking to themselves. She was bending down, pretending to work in the garden. In Italian she told me she had been working in the fields for hours and was tired. We went into the kitchen to get some juice, and it was then I noticed my grandmother making odd hand gestures. "Nonna, what are you doing?" I asked. "I am making pasta. Would you like to help me?" I sat down and together we made imaginary pasta. It was the last time I entered my grandmother's world of Alzheimer's, and as she smiled at me, I knew we had connected. Within minutes she had urinated all over her dress and broke out crying. The nurses took her away as I sat there, devastated by the few precious moments we had just shared.

At least once every two weeks I have the same dream. I am sitting in Nonna Bellini's kitchen amid a brilliant glow. The bright green-and-yellow flowered wallpaper lights up the room, and I can smell minestrone boiling on the stove. My grandfather is sitting in the living room on "his" chair, smoking a DuMaurier and watching *The Price Is Right*.

"You are alive," I say.

"Of course I'm alive," Nonna says, smiling at me.

"But I thought you were dead. I thought you had Alzheimer's," I say, delighted to see her healthy, strong and happy.

"No, I am alive and I will never leave you, Christina."

I smile back bursting with happiness. My Nonna Bellini will never die. She will always be there for me. Then I wake up crying, for Nonna Bellini died 12 years ago. My sadness over her death seems endless. When I go back to nothern Ontario during the holidays I still drive by the white-and-pink house on Kirby Avenue hoping that maybe she is still sitting in her living room, crocheting, *watchee teevee* and waiting for me to arrive.

I have come to understand more clearly the subversive and understated strength of womanhood. Women accomplish many things throughout their lives, but so much of it is taken for granted and not applauded as it should be.

⌐ HARRIETT GRANT

Lessons from Yea-Yea

HARRIETT GRANT

There is an old black-and-white photo in my family album of a smartly dressed middle-aged woman standing at the top of the front-porch stairs laughing at a little girl, whose back is turned to the camera. This is my grandmother, Clarissa Naomi Collins, at age 46, laughing at her granddaughter, Yola. My grandmother is now 83 and she is still laughing, but now she laughs at the antics of Yola's children. She has survived the Great Depression, two world wars, numerous personal dilemmas and emigration to Canada, all with her mind and sense of humour intact.

Born August 18, 1912, in Little London, Jamaica, Clarissa was the oldest of nine children, and one of four surviving girls born to Rachel and Fredrick Blake. She grew up in rural Jamaica, surrounded by sugar-cane plantations, and cared for her younger sisters while her parents worked on the nearby estates.

Her formal education ended when she reached age 14 because her parents could not afford to send her to high school, but she read and educated herself. In spite of her lack of formal education, my grandmother is rarely seen without a book or her bible in her hands. As a child I often found her asleep in bed, the bedside light on, her glasses half off her face, her mouth slack with sleep and her open bible clasped in her right hand.

When her formal education ended, my grandmother, like many young girls, was sent to a sewing mistress to learn to be a seamstress. At age 18, while working as a nanny, she met Bertram Grant and developed a friendship with him. This relationship ended soon after she gave birth to their son, her only child and my father, at age 21. She returned to live under the watchful eyes of her parents, who cared for her and kept her in the house until it was almost time for her to have her baby. She delivered her baby in a nearby town and returned home to her parents with her son.

My grandmother was a single parent with a son to feed and clothe, and had no source of support other than her parents. When my father was 11 months old, she left him with her parents and went back to work as a live-in nanny so that she could provide for him. In view of contemporary Canadian notions of the nuclear family, leaving your newborn child with your parents while you go to work elsewhere may seem unusual. However, in Jamaica, parents frequently have to leave children with grandparents and aunts while they go to the city or abroad to make a living and support their family back home. Once established in their new surroundings, the parents send for their children. My grandmother did this with my father, just as my parents did with me. At the age of 11 months, I was left with my grandmother in Jamaica when my parents moved to Canada.

When my grandmother visited my father as a child, he called her "Yea-Yea" instead of "Mama," because he called his grandmother mama. Like the rest of my immediate and extended family, I grew up calling my grandmother "Yea-Yea." However, since I lived with her for the first six years of my life, I thought of her as my mother, not my grandmother. She did not give birth to me nor did she breast-feed me, but she saw me safely through the thumb-sucking, dirt-eating, bed-wetting childhood stage.

For a young child a parent is someone who loves, protects, disciplines and guides; Yea-Yea did all these things for me. I bonded with her in a way that I have never bonded with my mother. In Jamaica I slept in a crib beside her bed, and on the many occasions when I wet my sheets, I would climb out of my crib and nudge her in her sleep until she woke. "Yea-Yea, I wet my bed" – this was all I had to say, and immediately she would change me and take me into her bed to sleep curled up next to her. My bedwetting may have been because I had to have my nightcap of Horlicks (a malted drink) and Ovaltine cookies before sleeping. As I sat at the kitchen table drinking my Horlicks, Yea-Yea soothed all my childhood fears about the headless horseman and "duppies" (ghosts) so that I felt safe and could sleep without nightmares.

My earliest memories revolve around my grandmother not only comforting but also scolding me. Like any child testing the limits of bad behaviour, I pushed the limits of Yea-Yea's patience until she took the switch to my skin to discipline me. "Spare the rod and spoil the child" is one biblical proverb Jamaicans take very seriously.

Yea-Yea had inherited property from her husband, and she leased out the land surrounding her house to young families, who built houses on it. There were always many children running around my grandmother's yard when I was a child. When I was not in my starched blue-and-white school uniform or my Sunday best, I was shaking mangoes off trees, climbing breadfruit trees, catching crabs before they could hide in their holes, and chasing boys. One afternoon, I chased a boy and hit him with a bamboo stick. I knew that I was going to face my grandmother's wrath once she discovered what I had done, so like the crabs I loved to catch, I hid underneath the house to avoid the fire of her switch. She found me, made me choose my own switch from the bushes in the yard, and gave me a spanking that I never forgot. I cried, but I understood why I was being spanked; I also knew that although she was the one who disciplined me, she was also the one who comforted me when I couldn't sleep or was scared.

When it was time for me to come to Canada, it was also time for Yea-

Yea to leave her home of 65 years and "live in foreign." Her only son was now successful enough to support all six of his children as well as Yea-Yea in Canada. I arrived at Malton International Airport on October 28, 1977, not knowing what I would be facing, but I knew that whatever it was, my grandmother would protect me.

In my new Canadian home, I had a mother, father, four brothers and a sister to provide for me, protect me and teach me to survive. Yea-Yea was no longer solely responsible for me; she could relax and become a grandmother. Our relationship changed as a result; nevertheless, I was still very attached to her. We shared a room and slept in the same bed until I was 15 years old.

As I became familiar with Toronto, I became Yea-Yea's faithful tour guide and guardian. It was my duty to help her get around on the subway, protect her from slipping on ice and to keep her company. In return she became my confidante; she knows things about me that my mother never will.

Although Yea-Yea was raised in an entirely different generation and culture than I was, she was open to change and seemed to understand my perspective. Unlike some grandparents who could not understand the "new generation," she allowed me to voice my fears and insecurities about my experiences as a Caribbean-Canadian woman of the "new generation." Most important, she always encouraged me with proverbs such as "Do what you can now while you are young." Regardless of the problems that I faced growing up in Canadian society, I knew that when I spoke to my grandmother, everything would be all right.

As I grew older, Yea-Yea became more frank with me about life. When I confessed to her my adolescent crushes or anything about my first boyfriend, she would remind me, "Get your education first." As a result of her many admonitions, I pushed myself hard to succeed academically; my expectations for myself were high because I did not want to disappoint Yea-Yea or the rest of my family. I had opportunities that she had never had, having grown up in Jamaica in the 1920s, and she expected me to take full advantage of all a Canadian education could offer.

Modern feminist thinking teaches young women to educate themselves, be financially independent and break down barriers to personal growth. However, I learned all these things from my grandmother while talking about my life and listening to the stories about her life.

At age 21, Yea-Yea as a young mother did not do the expected thing – marry the first man who came along who could support her and her baby. Instead, she chose to be financially autonomous and care for her child with the help of her family.

Yea-Yea views marriage as something that a woman commits to only after she accomplishes what she wants to do in life. As a young woman, she turned down many marriage proposals in favour of maintaining her independence. Yea-Yea finally married, at the ripe age of 44, to a nice gentleman named Mr. Collins, a wealthy widowed farmer with whom she had had a nine-year relationship; this alone was unconventional. On his deathbed, Mr. Collins married my grandmother to legitimize their relationship in the eyes of God. Yea-Yea claims that she married him to inherit his property and livestock; she felt she was entitled to it since she had stayed by his side during the last years of his life.

Yea-Yea talks of her husband without any trace of romantic notions. However, she gets dreamy eyed when she speaks of Bertram Grant, the father of her child. I believe that she does hold some romantic ideals, but she has never expressed them to me. Her advice is still, "Don't rush marriage," even though I have received a Master of Arts, a teaching certificate, and as a result, have a good career. She cautions me not to see marriage as the answer to my problems, not to bow to pressure from friends who are married and not to live up to other people's expectations. Strong familial ties enabled my grandmother to live independent of men. Family interdependence, grounded on female kinship, grants me the support and strength that I need to forge my own goals and succeed.

I had not always viewed my grandmother as wise or her advice as relevant. At 15, I demanded my own room and ended the nine years that I'd spent sleeping with my grandmother. Unlike my five-year-old self who had curled up next to her after nightmares about ghosts, I no longer felt that I needed my grandmother's protection. I was still close to Yea-Yea, she still knew most of my secrets and all of the major events in my life, but the dynamics of our relationship had changed. I did not seek her counsel as much as before; I now sought the naive and immature counsel of my adolescent friends. I was testing the waters of independence and saw my grandmother as a part of my Jamaican past.

During my adolescent years, I became fully assimilated into Canadian society. I shared similar "Canadian" values and experiences with my classmates, I spoke French regularly, coloured my speech with "eh," and talked about Wayne Gretzky and ice hockey. All traces of my Jamaican heritage were forgotten. I lost my Jamaican accent after two years of speech therapy to correct my childhood lisp. I didn't go to Caribana as other Jamaicans did, and I didn't tell friends about the rice and peas and ox tail that I ate at home. People assumed that I was Canadian born because of my speech and behaviour; if asked about my background, I said I was Canadian. In the media, Jamaican men were portrayed as drug dealers, murderers and steroid users; women as loud and abrasive sexual toys. The resulting stereotypes suggested that all druggies, thieves, murderers and teenage parents were of Jamaican descent. These were things with which I did not want to be associated; thus, I did not publicly identify myself as Jamaican.

However, in my second year at the University of Toronto, I attended a poetry reading by Lorna Goodison, a Jamaican poet, and this event changed my perspective on my cultural identity. Her poem "To Us All Flowers Are Roses," from her *Selected Poems,* evoked feelings of longing for the Jamaica of my childhood. The images her words formed in my mind had nothing to do with drug dealers and welfare mothers; she sparked within me feelings of cultural pride that had lain dormant for many years. As she recited her poems, I understood the sound, the phrasing, and her lilting lyrics transfixed me. I recognized the voice with which she spoke: it was my mother's voice, my grandmother's voice. It was the voice that I had lost. After hearing her, I was determined to reacquaint myself with my Jamaican past.

Culture is more than food, clothes and language; it is a way of thinking and feeling that lies at the core of your persona. I started my quest by talking with Yea-Yea, my direct link with Jamaican culture. Reading Anancy stories and Louise Bennett's "Jamaican Labrish" and "Aunty Roachie Seh" reminded me of my childhood. These Jamaican stories, poems and proverbs, which I read to Yea-Yea, depicted characters that escaped self-entrapment, left unhappy situations and cherished things they loved. Like the Maroons of early Jamaican history, they persevere in the face of despair. Reacquainting myself with Jamaican literature helped me reconcile my ancestry with the person I am today. I realize that I cannot let negative stereotypes about Jamaicans ruin my impression of Jamaica or make me ashamed of my background. Thankfully, Yea-Yea is still alive and has a great memory; she has helped me to reconcile my Jamaican heritage with my Canadian upbringing.

When I moved away from home at 18, I thought that I had learned all that I could from Yea-Yea's stories of her life. I went on with my own life, engrossed in my studies and unable to visit her regularly. I was an English major, and Virginia Woolfe and Maya Angelou were inspirational feminist models to me; their creative works exemplified the kind of feminist I wanted to become. In my last year of university, I raised my head from the books long enough to look around and realize what a *Phenomenal Woman* my grandmother truly was! I understood why her head never bowed; why she didn't have to shout, or jump about or talk loudly. Whenever I saw her, I felt proud, because she is a woman – phenomenally.

Today, Yea-Yea is 83 years old and still travelling. She goes to Jamaica for the winter and returns to Toronto in the spring. Because she is in her 80s and her health is slowly deteriorating, whenever she leaves I always pray that I will see her again in the spring.

This brings me once again to my childhood memories. When I was eight years old, my grandmother returned to Jamaica for the first time. The day of her departure, I stayed in our room alone and cried until my eyes were puffy. I had never been separated from her before and felt a great sense of loss. In 1982, when Yea-Yea came back from another long vacation in Jamaica, I was so thrilled that she had returned safely that I shed tears of joy when I saw her familiar face at the airport. People laughed at the spectacle, and my parents were actually embarrassed that I, a big 12-year-old girl, would not stop crying.

I no longer cry when my grandmother leaves for her annual vacation, but I always feel that sense of loss. Whenever I think of my grandmother's mortality, I remember that mournful day in my room. If I cried incessantly because she was going away on vacation, how would I react if I were never to see her face or hear her voice again? I don't know the answer to that question. I do know that I cherish every moment that I spend with Yea-Yea, and that her voice and smile will resonate within me.

In 1993, my grandmother was invited to Florida to visit her nephew and see her younger sister, Tan-Tan. I was compelled by love and nostalgia to arrange my schedule so that I could accompany her. When I had visited Jamaica two years before, I spent two days with Tan-Tan, and I was convinced that she and Yea-Yea were the same person. Tan-Tan fell asleep with her glasses on while reading her bible at night and she sang all the time, just as I recall my grandmother doing when I was younger. I thought it would be great to see the two of them together so I could find out if they were really the same person.

The reunion of the two sisters was wonderful; however, I soon realized that despite all their similarities, Yea-Yea and Tan-Tan were very different people. Like night and day, they share the sky but have different perspectives. Yea-Yea's sister is two years younger than her, but while my grandmother has a full head of grey hair, Tan-Tan's is naturally black. Tan-Tan sings and laughs constantly. Rather than acting to change the lot that life has thrown her, she thanks the good Lord and laughs. In comparison, if something or someone is bothering Yea-Yea, she will voice her concern and do something about it. She does not accept a bad situation; she acts to change it into something positive. What I admire most about my grandmother is that she does not give up. She devises strategies to overcome barriers and survive hardship with her mind and spirit intact.

When I returned from Florida, I had thought that I wanted to be just like Tan-Tan. She doesn't worry about anything but laughs and sings her problems away. However, more and more each day I realize that I am like Yea-Yea. I address my problems and make sure that my voice is heard, and then I do what I can to ease or remove the problem. I know now that I have a living example of the type of woman I want to be. I hope to be the phenomenal woman that Maya Angelou writes about – the phenomenal woman who is my grandmother.

Yea-Yea is not only a determined, outspoken woman, she is also vibrant and young at heart. I think that she resents the physical ailments that come with age; they only get in the way of her doing what she really wants to do. She always tells me, "Do all that you can when you are young, because when you are older you won't be able to do all the things you want." I try to live my life as Yea-Yea has lived hers – taking every opportunity to seize the day and realize my dreams. She does not see her perspective as extraordinary, considering her generation, neither does she see her life choices as unusual.

While working on this story, I asked Yea-Yea if she had any regrets. Would she make the same decisions if she had to live her life over again? She responded to me by saying, "I have no regrets, no regrets about anything." One day, I hope to look back on my life and utter those same words.

I bring Babcia's life into the lives of my sons. I tell them what strength and courage she had. I tell them with pride of their Polish heritage. I also teach them the value of diversity, and the importance of empathy and care for those who struggle every day to stay alive and sane. I remind them how fortunate they are to be Canadian, and how important it is to keep our doors open to those who suffer under the many hands of oppression.

⁓ HELEN (BAJOREK) MACDONALD

Grand [M]Other Tongue

HELEN (BAJOREK) MACDONALD

Under these words
Are the echoes of other words

— MARIA JASTRZESKA, quoted by Myrna Kostash in *Pens of Many Colours*

Dear Babcia:
In all those years we lived in the same household, I don't recall a single exchange of conversation with you. Mostly, I watched you. You watched me. Mostly, I ignored you. You forgave me.

I was the first child born into the home that was also hers. The rising sun pinches its way into my bedroom. From inside my flannel sheet cocoon I can hear her, down the hallway, roll to the side of her bed. The stiff mattress holds her firm while she pulls her brush through her long, grey, horsey hair. Brushing. Stroking. She stops, and I can see her, even with my eyes closed, weaving one strand over another, over and over and over in that ancient pattern until she arrives at the very bottom where she ties the thin end with an elastic. There's magic in the rapid whirling that winds her long braid to the base of her head, held there with a few pins. She then draws her night-gown over her head. The creaking of muscle and bone and the crackle of static and the crumple of fabric crush into my ears. Her bulky naked body begins its journey to the end of the hall to the large bathroom. Should I peak, or hide this morning? I burrow deeper into my cocoon.

The water is making its way through the pipes, gushing into the tub, drowning the sound of her private conversation. No one seems to know the character who flows from her imagination onto her tongue. The ever-present, yet quite absent, Mr. Karpinski puzzles me. Babcia frightens me. Intrigues me. Why is she like this? Different from my friends' grandmothers. Twelve years after my birth, her youngest grandchild, my baby sister, is born. Our house is busting at the corners with the crowding of nine bodies.

Another slumber party at a friend's house (never at my house). You know the kind. Pubescent best friends stay up all night playing "Truth or Dare," telling their deepest secrets, talking about the boys they like and about the girls they hate, the ones who actually need to wear a bra. Or gossiping about the one girl who must be easy because everyone knows she kisses with her mouth fully open! Where makeup tips and fashion tips are swapped and where fantasies of weddings and houses with picket fences and perfect children are mixed with the music of Donny Osmond, the Monkees and the Beatles. Where your best friends tell you they don't like to come to your house, because they are afraid of your grandmother. Babcia. One friend doesn't understand the words that come spitting out of her mouth in the foreign tongue. She mimics your babcia. Another complains that your babcia tried to kiss her once.

I used to blame our lack of communication on your inability to speak my language, my mother's language. You didn't take to my mother's tongue. You didn't like your son marrying that English tongue – not good enough for him! She couldn't offer the right kind of food for your son and his children. How could she? "Dat English no can cook!" Her brood was a pale sickly bunch, their cheeks hollow and colourless. How much your great hands ached to pinch the yellow of your Slavic ancestors into our flesh.

I had a limited grasp of your tongue, of my father's tongue, but I refused to engage with it. I was Canadian, not Polish. Canadians spoke English. "Speak English, Dad! Speak English, Babcia! When in Rome, or forever hold thy tongue." I ignored you. You forgave me.

It's so hard to love you when I hate your Polishness: your broken English and your old-country ways. It's the '60s and all my friends know the latest Polish jokes. A DP (Displaced Person) is a Dumb Polak . . . isn't it? It's hard to hate your Polishness when I love my aunt's galabki (cabbage rolls) and I like to dance with the Polish Girl Guides and sing Polish Christmas carols door to door. Old Polish men and women greet us at the door with tears and hugs of joy and treats born of old-country tradition. I hold fast to those parts of Polishness I like. But I don't go home to sing to Babcia, or even with Babcia. She doesn't seem to mind. She still gives me some chocolate.

Babcia, I used to blame the lack of communication on your craziness. That surgeon who incised a portion of your brain might as well have cut out your tongue. To alleviate the suffering of those around you, to control your mania when the shock treatments didn't work, to restrain your wild rebellion in this land of peace and freedom, the surgeon cut out what amounts to your heart, your soul and your tongue.

On that cold February day in 1960, nobody mourned the death of your vitality; rather, modern science heaved a sigh of relief. Another success story! Life is but one mode or another of existence. Relieved of your craziness (although everyone on our street whispered it prevailed), you were silent. I blamed your silence on your craziness.

I don't let on it hurts that my friends never come to my house. I don't have sleepovers because (I tell myself) there are too many people in the house already. I don't invite my friends over for supper because there isn't enough room left after nine family members sit at the kitchen table. There is barely enough food. Instead, I make fun of my babcia, just like my friends do. I make her sound scarier than they already imagine she is. I appropriate images of Old Baba Yaga, moulding into their minds images of fear and disgust. I tell them she swears a lot and waves her arms and sways in the chair she thinks is a rocker. One friend confides that she heard my babcia once chased the mailman away with a shovel, screaming at him in Polish. The neighbours called the police. I tell them how spooky it was to visit her at the Ontario Hospital, and how I could look at her only through bars in the windows. I try to erase the image of her tears as I mockingly tell them about the people at that place, some wandering about in pyjamas, staring past you as if you weren't there, others marching to imaginary music in the gardens, and the one who wore the paper bag over his head, singing foreign songs and talking to people you couldn't see. I try to forget all the others, sitting here and there, silent, looking out to where the water of the great lake meets the sky, pinching imagination into the flat horizon. In a whisper, I say that ever since she came back from the place with the barred windows, she talks to an imaginary friend. I think she talks about his . . . "you know." My friends listen intently, knowingly, imagining the thing I don't name. I tell my budding friends how large her breasts are. Yes, I see them naked, I tell them, and they are so huge she can wrap them around her big waist. "She's always walking around naked," I say, "and she's got hair 'there' too! It looks like a Brillo scouring pad." Their faces contort with disgust, then we all explode into giggling fits. Before long someone's parading around with toilet rolls as giant breasts, and my very best friend has found the Brillo pads. I laugh along with my friends as we all mock my babcia, toilet rolls and Brillo pads pressed comically to our bodies as I parade in burlesque fashion about my best friend's bedroom, singing a revised version of "Do your ears hang low?":

> *Do your tits hang low?*
> > *Do they wobble to-and-fro?*
> > *Can you tie 'em in a knot?*
> > *Can you tie 'em in a bow?*
> > *Can you throw 'em over your shoulder*
> > *in your over-the-shoulder-boulder-holder?*
> > *Do your tits hang low?*

I make it all up as I go, my crazy babcia's naked body the substance of my good time with my best friends. My best friend's older sister barges in, and advises us all to "grow up!" We mock her wiggle as she turns to leave.

The Babcia Burlesque has come to an abrupt end.

I used to blame your craziness on your refusal to accept the language and life of Canada. Your refusal to be Canadian. Your refusal to wrap yourself inside the maple leaf forever and close your eyes to your beloved white eagle. To accept would have meant killing your self – your Polish self – and, like a magician, imagining yourself of the new country: rebirth as a Canadian. Re-formed. No time to mourn for your dead. Someone I read – his name is Loriggio – calls this the acceptance of the "Canadianized mode of existence." But you wept. You rebelled. You refused to kill your Polish self. Your religion preached against suicide. It did not accept the myth of rebirth.

They punished you as if you were a traitor for not pledging allegiance to the soil beneath your feet. They didn't notice the Polish soil embedded under your fingernails. I noticed when I watched you braid your long, grey, horsey hair. I noticed when your hands reached for my cheeks upon which you longed to press your loving kisses.

Like a traitor, I refused to embrace my Polish heritage. I deserted you. I spurned you. I provided no light with which to help you find your way in a culture you could not understand. I left you perpetually in the dark about my life and its joys and sorrows. And now a crack of light enters the darkness that was my malice.

All day, each day since the operation in 1960, she sits in her chair, rocking to some ancient uterine rhythm, muttering in the foreign language of crazy people and in the foreign language of the old country. On wave upon wave of memory of the old country, she rises boisterously, then falls abruptly into silence. Sometimes, she presses her face into her hands, holding it there, compressing her foreign tongue into the gaps between her fingers, smothering the muffled sounds of her vitality.

Sometimes, she laughs. There is the laugh that mocks our mode of Canadianized existence. There is the laugh that drove into our ears shrill warnings of Old Baba Yaga hungrily seeking children in the dense forest of an old country. And there is that laugh, a suppressed laugh that comes from deep inside her belly, which her grandchildren had no words for – the laugh of her passions.

In my 14th year, you moved out, shuffled to the home of another of your children. Again, you lived in solitude with the blood of your Polish soil.

Babcia – how lonely you must have been, even in our house full of family! You were a foreigner in your own home. Foreign to your son's wife. Foreign to your son's children who denied you the simple pleasure of a loving kiss on sallow cheeks, yet greedily took the chocolates you offered on Sundays and holy days and any occasion you deemed special. And then, you died.

At your funeral, the tribe of Bajorek gathered. The priest sent you to your God in your own tongue. One of your grandsons remembered you in the foreign tongue of your adopted land. Did you hear him? Did you understand what he said?

He remembered your struggles to keep your family alive in Siberia, two and a half long years of death and disease and the repression of your language and your religion and your culture. But you had held fast. Your children would know where they come from. They would bleed the soil of their birth. How would they bleed!

He remembered your gathering of your brood, like Moses assembling the fold, in a country where they spoke Swahili.

He remembered the distant saviours in Great Britain who parted the red tape across the Atlantic Ocean so that you could go to Canada, that large pink mass of land, and start over again. It was 1949, and you would be a new woman. A modern woman. A beaten woman. A woman bleeding from her roots.

We all laughed at a few familiar anecdotes that told of your craziness. About the million-dollar house you would build to house all your children and grandchildren and great-grandchildren. One big happy Polish family, plus a few chickens and cows and pigs. We laughed through the tears.

And then, you returned to the soil. From under your fingernails, your reserve of Polish soil turned itself into the Canadian earth. Upon the Canadian landscape walk your grandchildren and great-grandchildren, all of whom are without [y]our tongue. Cut off by a mode of existence that marginalizes foreign tongues. That oppresses them. That oppressed you.

Dear Babcia, you suffered silently. Alone. And still you loved us inside your great hugs, your wet kisses, and with your kind heart. We were your son's children, and one day we would have our own children. More of you. And more time to remember . . .

I remember you – Victoria Rosalia Kotowicz Bajorek, survivor of the many hands of oppression. I tell my children about you, about your strength and your courage during those difficult years in the Siberian labour camp. I tell them we are all here, alive, free and much loved because of your will to live, to be free and to love.

You bet your *dupa* we come from the land of proud Poles!

Kiss me, Babcia, I'm Polish. *Daj buzi, Babcia, ja jestem Polak.*

I didn't permit myself the luxury of your loving kisses. I didn't make the time to talk with you. To talk in your tongue. Today I want to say, "Sit here a moment. I'll make us a cup of tea. Herbata. And we'll talk. Show me your tongue. Teach me."

Twoja Kochajaca Wnuczka,

Hela

Babcia died on January 5, 1992. As I looked upon her body, frozen in the permanent silence of death, I was flooded with memories, regrets and questions. It was too late to ask. Too late to apologize.

It was not too late to remember.

I remember more than just her craziness. I remember she was more than a mere peasant who landed like a wind-born seed on this land in 1949. I remember her strength, her pride, her devotion to her family and to her religion. I remember her love. I tell my children about Babcia, about her life.

It took years of stumbling through memory before I found Babcia. The heroine. And, indeed, she was!

I remember her . . .

My grandmother would not be considered a feminist in Japan, but in the western culture she is certainly viewed as one. She lived her life independently, demonstrating stength and an instinct for survival. I often feel I still need her wisdom.

━ NATSUKO KOKUBU

Obaachan: The Storyteller

NATSUKO KOKUBU

Obaachan, I miss you terribly.
I am a married woman now.
He is reliable, trustworthy, and he loves me.
Now, I have to lead my life without you.
If I could have one more moment with you,
I would whisper in your ear, ever so sweetly,
"Obaachan, I love you for all that you have given me,
especially your precious stories."
Your blood is my blood and your spirit dwells
inside me.
One day, I will give you a great-granddaughter.
She will be my daughter.
On her glorious birth, she shall inherit
all of those precious stories told to me by you,
Obaachan . . .

Tatsue Tanaka – Obaachan – was born into a wealthy Japanese family in a large city in Taiwan in 1903. She was the eldest of three sisters and had a happy childhood; unlike most people at that time, she and her family did not lack for material possessions. She also loved her parents, especially her father. The Tanakas controlled farmlands and ran a trading business in parts of east and southeast Asia, so her father had to travel extensively. She rarely got to spend time with him, but always eagerly awaited his return from business trips because he would shower her with gifts.

These were difficult times. Japan was attempting to conquer the Asian world, and many Japanese immigrated to Taiwan, China or elsewhere in Asia in search of a more prosperous future for their families. Obaachan's parents were no exception in this, nor did they escape the political turmoil that propelled Japanese immigrants back to Japan and left her father's business in tatters. Obaachan and her family lost touch with her father (though after a 30-year absence he quietly returned to them), and so Obaachan's mother was left to raise three young girls and run the family business single-handedly. By the time Obaachan turned eight, the new head of the family had had to claim personal bankruptcy and leave Japan temporarily.

Japan was destitute. Obaachan's mother and youngest sister suffered from cholera, but fortunately survived. Money was scarce, so the young Obaachan was forced to toil on farms, which as she had been born privileged, she wasn't accustomed to doing. She took a gamble and moved to the city, but conditions there proved even bleaker. Human rights were non-issues at this time, and Obaachan was exploited like so many other women and men. To eke out a living, Obaachan, now 12, was obliged to work in a factory. Each week she sent a substantial portion of her meagre salary to her family. It is no wonder she would later tell her grandchildren, "All luxury is an enemy. Save for our future Japan" – a perspective still shared by those who lived through the Great Depression. The Japanese mentality itself held that one does not live for oneself, but for one's country.

She continued to work until she was 16 or 17 and her family decided she should marry. Obaachan often recounted that my grandfather was a good husband; a man she could rely on. She considered reliability in a husband a characteristic superior to love, as it is a reliable man and not a hopeless romantic who will successfully provide for a woman and her children. The Japanese still tend to regard marriage as a partnership, an investment for the future. While this may seem practical and calculating, I too believe it to be true.

The two world wars called for vast numbers of troops, so women aspired to give birth to healthy boys. Obaachan had eight children but only one boy, who was born after the Second World War. A woman's inability to conceive boys was a source of embarrassment; such women were thought to be unpatriotic and they faced discrimination. Obaachan could not tolerate this injustice, and said she was grateful my grandfather did not endorse these views either. Shortly after the Second World War, Obaachan lost her husband, but there was precious little time to grieve because she had to tend to her large brood. Food was hard to come by, and daily necessities were fully controlled by the government. Money was substituted for food stamps, which were still not sufficient to provide sustenance for hungry families. But her arduous life only succeeded in strengthening her resolve and sharpening her wisdom.

Perhaps by North American standards Obaachan would be considered a feminist, but I believe that she, like many other women, was primarily a true survivor. In Japanese culture it is the women who have an innate sense of self, though Japanese women were blatantly treated as the inferiors of men, who wielded power in both the private and public domains. For instance, men could seek divorce if their wives failed to bear male children, but women who suffered physical abuse at the hands of their spouses did not have the same option. This explains one reason why Obaachan was so fond of her husband.

Obaachan was a wonderful teacher. She would say, "Being a winner does not mean destroying others in the process. Everyone has good and bad things in life, just like daylight and night. So, one should accept life as it is." During my melancholic moments, she would console me with her tales. When, at the age of eight, I was sad over the loss of my pet, Obaachan told me that the memories of loved ones should be cherished even though the time we share with them is cut short.

My mother always said I was Obaachan's favourite because she was present at my birth. My father was away on a business trip during the delivery. My mother knew she was in safe hands, though, because Obaachan was a midwife. (During both world wars, midwives took over after most doctors were sent to the battlefields.) She actually assisted the doctor with the delivery and was the first relative to hold me in her arms and whisper Japanese lullabies to me as she washed me tenderly. But each time I broached the subject of my birth with her, Obaachan would casually reply, "It is an obligation for women to help each other."

I know my mother also derived a considerable amount of knowledge from her mother. As a result of Obaachan's hardships, my mother learned that women can survive without men. My mother, even after several years of marriage, is a self-made woman.

Oftentimes, Obaachan's notion of independence was intimidating. If I compare my life with hers, I feel she is far stronger than I will ever be. It would be inconceivable for me to live 60 years of my life without a partner, as she did, or to live alone during my golden years despite the fact that my family – just a few blocks away – pleads with me to move in with them. Alas, solitude became Obaachan's faithful and sole companion.

As a Japanese-Canadian woman, I learned to accept help from my loved ones while retaining my independence. As much as honour, respect and pride are commendable traits, I do not take pride to an extreme because I witnessed the negative impact it had on my grandmother.

When she was ailing, my elderly Obaachan did not ask for assistance from either her children or grandchildren, though she suffered from diabetes, which would sometimes render her unconscious. We said we could not care for her properly unless she lived with us, but she rejected these countless offers of hospitality. My grandmother never came to our home for extended visits without a valid reason. She would willingly stay over to nurse my sister and me during our bouts of illness (mine were more frequent) because this made her useful and not an inconvenience or nuisance. I relished her company. I'm convinced her anecdotes were the ultimate remedy:

> One day, a man lost his way home.
> It was getting darker and darker.
> All of a sudden, he saw flowers in an open place.
> They were so beautiful that it touched his heart.
> From nowhere, another old man in white appeared and told him:
> "Do you know the flowers called 'kindness?'
> If you don't, look at these.
> See.
> The red bud opens.
> The hungry little boy gives up his milk for his younger brother.
> Look at the yellow bud with tears.
> A girl gives up receiving cloth for matsuri
> because she knows her parents are poor,
> and it is impossible to buy cloth for the two children in the family.
> Her little sister is happy with the new dress
> and she is crying in her mind.
> The tears you see are hers.
> When someone sacrifices for others, flowers are born.
> When someone sacrifices his or her life, mountains are born."
> When he found the old man it all disappeared,
> he was in the place he knew again.
> The flowers and mountains disappeared,
> and he never had a chance to see them again.

*   *   *

Once upon a time, there was an old man and an old lady.

They worked hard, but they were poor.

One day, the old man went to the mountain to get some bamboo to make baskets.

While he was cutting the bamboo, he came across one that was different from the rest; this one was shining like gold.

When he cut the bamboo, he found a little girl sitting inside it.

The old man took the little girl home.

This couple had no children.

They took care of her as their very own.

From that point on, each time he cut bamboo, he found money inside so he could feed the little girl.

Shortly after, they became rich.

The little girl turned into a beautiful woman.

Her beauty mesmerized all the charming men.

Even the king fell in love with her beauty.

She rejected all of her suitors.

The men wondered why.

On the day of the full moon, the people from the village wondered why she cried helplessly, gazing at the moon far away.

She was prepared to confess her true origin.

She was born from the moon.

She must now return to her home.

All the people were surprised and asked the king to prevent her from returning home.

They loved her and didn't want to lose her.

They prepared an army to fight the people from the moon.

Suddenly, a bright light appeared that blinded everyone,

except the old man, the old woman and the girl.

The people from the moon

thanked the old man and old woman for taking care of the girl.

"We will never forget you."

In Japanese culture, these short tales carry a special meaning. They are whispers of wisdom, voiced by my great-grandmother to be passed down to my grandchildren some day. They bespeak human experience and form an intergenerational link between my Obaachan and me.

One day, my grandmother asked her family to accompany her to the hospital. No questions were asked, but we quickly came to understand why we were there. Obaachan's days were numbered: her blood-sugar level was too high. She was virtually blind, and for the first time in her life, she was lying motionless in a hospital bed. She succumbed to her disease a few months later. I was not by Obaachan's bedside at the time of her death, and for this, I will always feel guilty. Obaachan died as she lived – with dignity. We mourned her passing for a long time. To this day, I cannot help but wonder whether she would have been happier and healthier living with us, but her pride was a hurdle we could never overcome.

As a Japanese-Canadian woman, I have discovered there is no shame in expressing a need for others, and thus I feel inclined to re-evaluate the customs and beliefs of the "old country." Like many others, I depend on the media, technology, academia, peers and loved ones' knowledge and direction. As a wife, I often turn to my husband for support, love and compassion. As a feminist, I am committed to helping other marginalized groups (women, in particular) deal with the cultural issues with which I am forever grappling.

My physical appearance apparently mirrors that of my grandmother: from my oval-shaped eyes to the texture of my jet-black hair, to my sweet smile and gentle voice. Some of her old friends claim I have adopted my grandmother's graceful gait as well. I can only hope I have inherited Obaachan's unique spirit.

Writing about my grandmother consolidated my under-standing of the heroism of ordinary women's lives. The process of writing revealed the depth of my outrage – that my rich cultural history has oftentimes been diminished to perogis and pisanki.

— ALYS MURPHY

Keeper of the Kopek

ALYS MURPHY

The house is storybook picturesque – roof thickly thatched, walls clayed and whitewashed every spring during "turnout." Bright sunflowers bloom around the doorway. A white cat purrs in the sunlight. Fruit hangs heavy in the trees beside the house. A woman sits on the threshold finishing stitches on the *perena,* a feather mattress, on her lap.

An idyllic setting. It belies reality. War rumours fly, and Nastasya has taken the precaution of sewing her only money into the *perena* – one truly pitiful kopek coin, worth less than a cent. Her youngest child, small and barefoot, hovers, surreptitiously stroking the soft skin of her cheek and her mother's lustrous dark braid, which when unbound for combing, sweeps the ground. The little one stores up these pleasures against the time when Mama goes away again, leaving her own children for days or weeks, to help strangers give birth to theirs.

"Marenya, if I'm not here, take this with you. Keep it with you."

"Yes, Mama."

The war – the First World War – descends upon them. Prewar hunger and deprivation become starvation and terror. The purring white cat, enticed by starving soldiers billeted in the storybook cottage, becomes soup. They offer to share it with Marenya. For the rest of her life she can't bear to be near a white cat.

In 1918, when Marenya is eleven, Nastasya dies of typhus.

When Marenya is almost 16, she takes the *perena* and her eldest sister's passport and leaves the storybook cottage forever. Alone.

Canada changes Marenya to Mary, sometimes even to Molly. She has two daughters, Nadya and Lesya. Their names are too foreign for white folks, and outside the Ukrainian community they are Lillian and Alys. They take heed and name their daughters Jane, Joan, Sandra and Shannon.

Nastasya's foremothers, the indigenous women of the Ukraine, had lived on the steppes and by the rivers for at least half a million years. For those hundreds of millennia, like all people of the land, their lives were guided by the changes of the seasons and the moon, the cycles of planting, growth, harvest, fallow, birth, celebration, death and remembrance. Their ancient customs, based on these implacable rhythms, survived into the 20th century.

Comparatively inconsequential events, such as the imposition of Christianity or the waves of invaders that swept over the land, were absorbed into these old customs: Christianity was practised in public, but at home most women continued their old ways. They talked to the bees, honoured the ancestors and included them in family celebrations, practised divination at the turn of the seasons and welcomed strangers, extending hospitality with bread and salt. In thousands of other small ways, sometimes thinly veiled, more often not, they carried on their oral traditions, telling their daughters the proper way of things.

The sperm of the invaders got absorbed into their bodies. That this is so is evident in the ancient African names of my mother and myself, now common Ukrainian names, and in the Mongol and Manchurian features of our faces, and in my own full lips.

Change came slowly to the people then, if it came at all. Those who left the steppes and the rivers took the memories of the old ways with them, frozen in time. When my mother and my sister Nadya visited Poland in the 1970s, people were fascinated by their Ukrainian: Mama and Nadya were told they spoke the Ukrainian equivalent to Elizabethan English. And whenever I move house, the sacred bread and salt precede me. They create an energy in the new house that modifies or enhances the existing spirit. My daughter does the same. We talk to our animal companions with respect, conscious of their generous contribution to our well-being. Inclusion of a plate for ancestors at our family celebrations affirms awareness of our connection to the lives of those who came before us.

My baba, Nastasya, was born near Skalat in Halychena. In those days, the word "Ukraine" was not used – that is 20th-century recent. Intellectuals called the land Rus. Simple people, land people, "belonged to" or were "family of" Halichane, Bukovinchi, Hutsule, Lehmke; *narodny* – compatriot – translates literally as "family" or "of the same birth." These people were descendants of the seven original indigenous tribes. Nastasya's foremothers were *korovody,* the tribe of ceremonialists.

Baba was born Nastasya Zahaidak. Her mother's last name had been Svestuyn, which was probably the matriarchal clan name (a *svestuyn* is a whistler). In Halychena, the family names and worldly goods of serfs and peasants were passed on matrilineally until sometime in the 19th century. Hanjka, my mother's sister, inherited the storybook cottage and the two morgs of land after the First World War in keeping with this custom.

It is likely that my baba was born a serf. In theory, serfs were emancipated in 1861; in fact, Nastasya lived her whole life in serfdom. A friend of my mother's recalls having seen a *khlop* (slave) exchanged for a hunting dog by two of the local *pane* (landowners) at a *yarmarok* (village marketplace) in 1910.

Nastasya married Pyietro Khotan and raised five children: Ivan, Vasyl, Teklya, Hanjka and Marenya. Marenya was more than 20 years younger than Ivan. Pyietro, restless by nature, was rarely around to tend their two morgs of land and eventually left to try his luck on the fabled streets of gold in a place called Canada. All the villagers were convinced he would be swallowed up by the sea monsters that inhabited the oceans. Marenya was three when he returned, and she recalls the great excitement upon word that her father was coming back. She has told of her unbearable delight in anticipation of his return, and her subsequent bitter devastation. He never once touched, looked at, or acknowledged her. I wonder if my mother was a child of loneliness. She was certainly different from the others – brilliant, intrepid – and Baba had had to walk alone to distant villages. It was only a matter of time before Pyietro left again for Canada, this time never to return, leaving Nastasya and the children to fend for themselves.

When Marenya was small, she caught diphtheria. Nastasya bound her up in wrappings soaked in water and sprinkled with the scrapings of crude sulpha, and kept her for three days on the heated *pietz,* a tiled stove with broad shelves for sleeping. Marenya survived, without losing her hair. Her skin, however, all peeled off.

Centuries of mass murder virtually eliminated women healers, but the Inquisition never reached Skalat. Wise women lived and passed their terrestrial ways on to their daughters and their daughters' daughters. Nastasya was a midwife and the unofficial doctor to villages for miles around. She knew about herbs, birthing, abortion and healing rituals, and eventually she instructed Marenya in these skills. In time, my sister became a public health nurse and doctor of acupuncture, and I a wholistic counsellor to women. Without conscious intent, we have continued to heal.

Nastasya kept the old ways, and was never paid in money for her services. The mother of a new child would pay her with a kerchief or an apron, and sometimes with food. In keeping with tradition, if the birth was untroubled, Nastasya would stay with the new mother for three days, and on the third day, would perform the infant's ritual hair clipping and bath with the prescribed sacred herbs.

Baba also had skills as a cook, which the village priest and local nobility sought for their banquets and celebrations. The gentry expected free service from the serfs, so it never occurred to them to pay Baba. Food that remained after the feast was left for the following day, or was fed to the pigs. But somehow, Nastasya never returned home to her children without white bread or sweet cakes, which found their way into the voluminous top of her *sorochka,* a calf-length dress over which a skirt and apron were worn. When Baba discovered that the priest and his family ate meat clandestinely during lent, she fed her own children whatever was available, insisting it was her responsibility to follow the priest's good example.

I never knew my baba. I have never seen a picture of her and do not know if one even exists. My knowledge of her comes from the stories my mama told me over and over. My mama mourned Baba until her own death at age 73. Some of what I know comes from the memories of others from the village, those who survived the First World War, the flu and typhus epidemics of 1918, and the heartbreak of a hostile Canada, where they found destitution, exploitation and internment in Canadian concentration camps. And some of what I know about Baba and her circumstances comes from my research on Halychian history and folklore. I turned to the research and the writing of this story when I no longer wanted to erase my past. Those who came before me are an integral part of who I am today.

What would Nastasya say to see her name in print?

The year is 1982. The perena *has long since been taken apart and made into pillows. My mama died two years ago, and now I am the keeper of the kopek, entrusted to pass it, with its story, to my own precious daughter.*

Six o'clock at the end of a dull, snowy day. Home from work. I approach my suburban bungalow, which is trite and uniform rather than picturesque, and even before I enter I sense something is wrong.

The house has been violated. Tumbled. Ransacked. Things have been taken. Some things, things that insurance companies value, can be bought and replaced.

The kopek is gone.

Yiayia was my vital link to the Greek language and to religion. Any connection I have with my mother tongue came through my grandmother. She showed me the force of the imagination through the games we played and the stories she told. She also taught me about the power of faith. For her, faith was the ability to believe in things that cannot be easily seen or measured. I have become who I am by learning who she was. Yiayia was my vital link to the place from which I come.

— ELPIDA MORFETAS

Yiayia's Whispered Prayers

ELPIDA MORFETAS

Yiayia, my grandmother, and I came to this country together as immigrants. Hand-in-hand, she, a 60-year-old woman, and I, a two-year-old girl, left the plane and stepped into Canada, May 27, 1971. Years later she told me that she was scared; she did not speak any English, except for a handful of words such as "No English, Greek." She had not been able to learn much more than this, as her adult children and her failing health kept her close to their homes. At the time of our arrival, I thought that the small, olive-skinned, grey-haired, full-figured woman with whom I travelled was my mother. I did not know that my "real" mother, who had left Greece the year after I was born, was waiting for me and that Yiayia was bringing me to her. On the day of our arrival, Yiayia was wearing her navy-blue dress with the small white polka dots and her soft, black suede shoes. Her hair was short; she tamed the loose strands with hairpins tucked over each ear. She smelled like lemons and warm honey. I buried my face in Yiayia's lap when I met my mother; I did not know this strange woman. Yiayia was not particularly fond of my mother, a daughter-in-law who came from a remote island village, and so she secretly chose to break my strong attachment to her very slowly.

In Canada Yiayia's role was that of caregiver; she took care of all her grandchildren as our parents worked long hours. She cooked and even cleaned the houses of her children during her first years in Canada. She had a weakness for her grandchildren; she spoiled us and dealt out very lenient punishments. Being the eldest granddaughter, I never experienced any of her punishments. In my early childhood she gave me so many sweets that my teeth were beginning to rot even before they were fully in place.

Yiayia used food as an expression of her love. Perhaps her feelings about food resulted from her struggles during the Second World War and the Greek Civil War. She had come from a poor family and was orphaned at an early age, and then Papou, my grandfather, died just before he turned 50, leaving her to raise their three children alone. She probably felt overburdened with guilt when she could not feed them regularly. Food became a prize that was usually won only after a hard struggle. Throughout her life, she would continue to hoard, praise and often think of food. Eating became a passion and a compulsion for her. When Yiayia was living with us, my mother and I would empty bruised, purple plums, bits of crusty bread, raisins and various other tiny portions of food from the pockets of her cotton dresses before washing them. Yiayia used food to calm herself in moments of panic and to appease her children and grandchildren.

Her love of food and feeding others seemed naturally to make her an exquisite cook. She taught her husband, her daughters and my mother to cook every Greek dish imaginable. She began to teach me too. As she grew older and her body was losing its former strength and agility, she would sit at the kitchen table and offer advice and guidance while others duplicated her recipes: *koulourakia, kourabiedes* and *melomakarona* at Christmas, sweetbread at Easter and my papou's favourite hot-and-red dish, a secret recipe brought over from Smyrna. In Greek culture, food is tied to every significant event in life and its celebrations: birth, death, Christmas and Easter. With her strong arms, Yiayia would knead sweetbread dough for half an hour, then weave it into intricate designs, glaze it with egg yolk and decorate it with an egg, dyed red for Easter, symbolizing Christ's blood. She taught these and other traditions to her family.

When Yiayia came to Canada she stayed with my family and her youngest daughter's family. Her eldest daughter lived in Athens, and she would often send money to her and cry whenever they spoke on the telephone. The two families in Canada divided her between them; as a result, she switched houses every few months. She did not like moving her things from one house to the other, but she had difficulty deciding with which family she wished to live permanently. She felt this would mean choosing among her children and grandchildren. Besides, by alternating households she probably felt she could keep an eye on everyone.

Whenever she moved away from our house, I would help her pack her things. While we prepared her clothes, Yiayia would tell me stories of her girlhood and her life in Greece. She had no photographs that proved how she had looked and lived, but she did have stories. If you tried to investigate her life through pictures you would find that most of Yiayia's pictures are of her with her husband and babies. But she had a life before any of us were born.

My yiayia was born January 1, 1911, a New Year's baby, a very lucky time to be born. Her birthplace is a dry and barren rock island called Syros. She was the third of five children. Her father, George Dapola, a Greek of Italian descent, died when Yiayia was only a few months old. Her mother was a Greek woman named Maria Paleologos. Paleologos means "old words or pre-words"; Yiayia said it was the name of the Byzantine emperors and empresses. Yiayia was always proud of her mother's name and her Greek heritage. Her first name, Elpitha, is Greek for hope. She would say to her grandchildren, "I am Esperanza in Spanish, in French I am Esperance and Elpitha in Greek."

When she was nine or ten years old, my yiayia's nona (godmother), paid for her to go to a boarding school run by Catholic nuns on Syros.

Her nona believed it was necessary for the girl to learn a *techni*. Girls of my yiayia's time and social class were taught to survive by earning a living as a garment worker, seamstress, cook, maid or nanny. At this school they were taught basic writing, arithmetic and French. They were also taught the Roman Catholic religion in a nation of people whose religion was predominately Christian Orthodox.

The school was actually a charity school, a working orphanage in an old grey stone building overlooking the Mediterranean Sea. The nuns were strict; the girls' blue-and-white uniforms and caps had to be clean and neatly arranged on their bodies at all times. The food was tasteless and meagre. Young girls who had no families to look after them were sent here.

I think that my yiayia must have stood out; she was a rebellious child. She wore her cap backwards. The nuns always insisted that shoes had to be arranged outside the dormitories by size and colour; black for the older girls and brown for the younger ones. Once, Yiayia and her friend Alessandra rearranged the shoes: a tiny brown shoe was placed beside a village girl's very large black one; a left was placed by another left, and so on. The girls woke up at five o'clock the next morning, and there was chaos; chasing and arguing over who had what shoe, while Yiayia and Alessandra stood in the corner and laughed. But Yiayia suddenly felt herself being painfully lifted off the ground by her thick, frizzy, dark-brown hair, which was in the grasp of an angry nun behind her. She and her friend were punished: they had to polish all the shoes.

Still, this did not deter them, and they sought for more gratifying ways to break the monotony of the school day. One late afternoon, when all of Greece retires for a nap, the two friends managed to unlock the heavily barred iron doors of the school and then raced out for a swim while the other girls were praying or reading in their rooms. The school forbade the girls to swim or wander along the seashore; the nuns considered this time wasted. Alessandra and Yiayia ran down the pathway from the school's side door to the beach. Alessandra stood on a rock and screamed: "A Greek who can't swim is like a dead fish on the shore!" Then she took off her uniform and jumped into the water. Yiayia laughed and loosened her hair, then followed Alessandra into the sea. Yiayia loved Alessandra and thought of her as a true poet because Alessandra loved freedom and adventure. They swam and played in the waves; in the sea they were mermaids, fish, octopuses, whales and sharks, and on the shore they were pirates and sea captains.

It was not until their third excursion that they were caught. One of the girls at the school was very ill, and two worried nuns wandered the hallways trying to deal with the newly arisen crisis. They happened to glance through the school's bay windows and recognized the girls, who were sun-bathing naked on a large rock. The nuns both screamed. The girls were dragged into the school, and another punishment followed – this one more severe than the last. Yiayia's oldest sister, Teresa, who had raised Yiayia and her siblings since their mother's death, was blamed for bringing up such an *adespoto* child: the girl was fearless, headstrong and truly ungovernable. The two friends were lectured, spanked, given extra duties and made to say penance in front of the whole school. Then they were separated.

I know this story well because Yiayia told it to me over and over again. It was delicious to hear because I felt my own misbehaviour as a child could be traced back to it and justified.

Yiayia's short time at this Catholic school was the extent of her formal education; soon after this incident she was permanently withdrawn from the school. However, Yiayia's lack of education did not mean she held lit-tle respect for "book smarts." She insisted that her children and grand-children be educated; "Become someone," she said. While she was living with us, she encouraged my sisters and I to do well in school, and not only in Greek school but English school as well. When my mother was busy or tired, it was Yiayia who helped me with my Greek-school home-work. I read my assigned passages to her, and she would correct my pro-nunciation. While standing on a chair, I recited special Independence Day poems for her. Every week our teacher assigned essays that we had to write in Greek, and I even read these to her. Yiayia carefully criticized my work: "too boring," "not enough description," "that's not true," she would say. But sometimes I would get "very good" out of her. Once she asked, "Why doesn't this teacher ask you to write something about your yiayia?" after a composition called "*E Papoudes mas*," (Our Grandfathers) had been assigned, which was supposed to detail how our grandfathers had influenced history. Still, Yiayia obliged and gave me the details of my papou's life and what he meant to her.

Unfortunately, Yiayia could not help me to the same extent in English school. She had to find other ways to show her support and ensure our success: she used her favourite saints. Yiayia wore a sterling silver chain around her neck, upon which hung various small charms. Some of these pieces were portraits of various Catholic and Greek Orthodox saints, while others had details of these saints in action. There was Saint George on his horse, slaying a dragon; Saint Nick protecting fishermen whose boat was about to crash on a large rock; and even a small key to the Virgin's heart. Yiayia also had a charm depicting a Mohawk woman, Kateri Tekakwitha, a martyred saint who had been converted to Christianity long ago. She had long braids and held a large wooden cross over her chest. A layer of clear blue covered the saint's portrait, which made her look like she was holding her breath under water. If anyone had trouble buying Yiayia a gift, they would just get her a religious charm to hang on the chain around her neck.

I remember Yiayia giving me this necklace each time I wrote exams in high school. Yiayia knew I could pass my exams without it, but wearing the necklace would give me an extra push to do well. I was embarrassed to wear the rusty-looking silver chain outside my clothing, so as soon as I left the house I quickly shoved the charms inside my shirt, where they hung, cold and heavy. Yiayia also stuffed a small icon and a jar of holy water into my backpack, and warned me that these would bring me luck only if I kept the bag nearby while I was writing. I tried to explain that all bags had to be put at the front or side of the room to ensure we would not cheat. Yiayia said, "So, sit by the wall. If you don't, the protection will go to someone else." I did not want to hurt her feelings, so I did as she said. Yiayia saw these objects as holy relics invested with powers to protect against all kinds of evil. Years later, I discovered that in the Greek

Orthodox church, religious icons are like windows to heaven that allow the believer to have contact with otherworldly beings. Yiayia believed in the visions she saw through these windows, but also in the power of introspection and private prayer. She had her own private church in a corner of her room.

There were few rituals that Yiayia followed as diligently as that of prayer. I could not speak to her during her nightly prayers, but I was allowed to sit on her bed and watch as she chanted long prayers by memory before a small tin icon of the Virgin holding a baby Jesus. A small red bulb illuminated their faces. She faced this electric icon, straightened her back as much as possible, held her walking cane with both hands and leaned it against her stomach. Then with eyes half-closed, she would say her prayers in a low, whispering voice. She said words with many "th" sounds in them, perhaps because the word for God in Greek is *Thaio*. Once, she tried to teach me the Lord's Prayer in Greek. I could never remember all of it, only the first and last lines, but she let me get away with mumbling the rest.

During the summer when I was nine, Yiayia went back to Greece to visit her other daughter and friends. I would go to her room and pray to the electric icon. I noticed that it would not often grant wishes. Before she left for Greece I asked her, "Yiayia, what should I think of when I'm in Church?" She surprised me with a serious answer: "Never think of the Devil." After this, of course, images of the Devil crept into my thoughts, but he was not so much threatening as mischievous. My illusions were probably instigated by the combination of having to stand in a hot, poorly ventilated church around lighted candles and the ritual of fasting before taking communion. Being in a hallucinatory state, I thought I was seeing the Devil; he stood in the corner and made faces at the priest, laughed as he carelessly peeled the paint off the icons, and painted mustaches on the female saints. These female saints wore long gowns with no bulges and their faces housed sunken eyes and hollow cheeks. Even without mustaches, the women's faces resembled the bearded faces of the male saints.

Beside the images of these saints, I saw the full-grown female body of my yiayia. Her body had survived many trials but it was still matronly and beautiful. During her last years she would call on me to help her dress. After she had suffered two strokes she could not even reach to fasten or unfasten the hooks on her bra. I would arrange her dress and undergarments on her bed while she was bathing. Then, she would call on me to help her dress and comb her hair. Lastly, I would squeeze her small swollen feet into her soft suede shoes. I could not see her likeness in the classical statues of ancient Greece that worshipped youth, but when I saw the small, headless statues of prehistoric earth goddesses, I thought of my yiayia: body shaped like a pear, small shoulders with heavy breasts, large belly and wide hips.

Sometimes it was hard for me to match the older woman who sat telling stories with the girl who dressed up, thumbed her nose at nuns, cheated a German officer for food during the war, and approached any man who pleased her for a date. Before the war, Yiayia worked as a counter girl at a pastry shop. She tied up her dark hair in intricately woven braids; she used black paint to create a beauty mark on her left cheek and she painted her lips red. I have heard that Papou was the delivery boy who dropped all the eggs he was carrying the first time he saw her. There were some connections Yiayia had with this young woman from the past: the shine in her eyes when she spoke of my papou and her old friends, her sense of humour, her challenging nature. Her stories ensured that I would remember who she had been as a girl and woman before she became my yiayia.

Other than being a good storyteller, she was a healer and protector of the family. She spoke mystical chants and made the sign of the cross in the air above us. Night after night, as my sisters and I slept, Yiayia would creep into our room and make this sign above us to ensure good dreams. She knew home remedies to cure the likes of burns, headaches, stomach aches and depression. Together we also healed animals. We once found a pigeon struggling with a wounded wing in our garden. Yiayia helped me wash the wound and stop the bleeding with tobacco from an unrolled cigarette. We found a cardboard box and filled it with straw. The pigeon cooed and opened and closed its eyes in the dark. Three days later it flew away.

When I was 16, Yiayia died at the age of 74; her liver stopped working and her lungs filled with fluid. She died in a hospital far away from us. Greeks believe that children should never be exposed to death in any form, and so her grandchildren were not allowed to be near her when she was dying.

Before she entered the hospital for the last time, she gave me her wedding ring and insisted I keep it in memory of her. Yiayia's death ended my childish notion that good things can go on forever. I walked around in a state of numbness at her funeral. I did not cry, but eventually broke down at home when my aunts and I had difficulty lighting the *kandili*, a small lantern that is supposed to guide the dead person's soul until it is called into the afterlife.

Yiayia was our escape in our parents' house. She was different from the other Greek women in our family: she seldom spoke of growing up or of us children being married someday. She taught us by telling stories, playing games and vetoing my father's calls for punishment. After a life of hard realities, she relinquished the traditional role of overbearing matriarch. After her death, whenever I felt I was being swallowed up by problems at school or with my parents, I would go to her room and sit on her bed to feel her protective presence.

Yiayia was a survivor, an inventor and a dreamer. In the summer, she would sit for long spans of time, on the porch or in her preferred place among the flowers of my mother's garden. Leaning her chin on her cane, she would gently close her eyes, and her mind seemed very far away. The sun made her brown, wrinkled face glow, while bees and butterflies, her beloved creatures, swirled around her.

My yiayia placed great importance on names and naming. In Greek culture names are passed from one generation to the next; children are obliged to pass on their parents' names, and grandparents bestow their names on their grandchildren. Yiayia never allowed my name to be translated from Elpida to Hope, because she feared I would lose my connection to her, to the Greek language and culture. When I was a child it seemed an unnecessary burden to carry a name outside its native country; a name no one could remember or even pronounce. Knowing for whom I was named gave me some solace and inspired pride in the uniqueness of this name.

Yiayia would say, "We are the daughters of Sophia. We are Hope, Faith and Love. These are the most beautiful things on this earth."

My mother had given me my paternal yiayia's name in order to secure her mother-in-law's approval: she did it to demonstrate that she was a dutiful daughter-in-law. I was born in Athens the summer that my yiayia was 58 years old. She dressed in black at the time, like many widows in the Mediterranean, although my papou had died more than 10 years beforehand. Many days passed before my yiayia came to see me. I am told that she was very happy the day I spoke my first words, which my mother says was surprisingly early. Maybe Yiayia hesitated and then came when she was sure her name and stories would live on in me.

Women's history has taken place mostly in the private sphere, and as such has been largely ignored. The fact that this book focuses on older women is critical. It is a contribution to a vastly underrepresented subject. The value of older women as sources of wisdom has been overlooked. This collection pays tribute to that value.

— NICOLA LYLE

Sit on a Cushion, Sew a Fine Seam

NICOLA LYLE

At my mother's urging, my grandmother wrote her autobiography in 1985 at the age of 70. The last time I saw Gran in Northern Ireland, I had the opportunity to read about her life experiences. I was 17, and her words both disturbed and moved me. Her life was a combination of the painful, the arduous, the joyous and the passionate. The parallels between her childhood and my own startled me, and our common experiences allowed me to share secrets that would otherwise have remained undivulged. Her story allowed me to understand her as a person, outside her role as my grandmother. When she let me read her words that fateful night in Ireland, it was an act sacrosanct to us both; a recognition of her trust in me and an acknowledgement that I was old enough to discover several truths about her.

When I learned of my grandmother's death, I was in Canada. I automatically thought of the autobiography and Gran's diaries. I asked my grandfather to locate and safeguard the boxes containing the precious texts until my next visit to Ireland. I had no idea what a foray into the past would trigger, but I knew that my grandmother's story would not go untold.

Elizabeth "Lily" Vogan Moore was born in 1915. She was very close to her own grandmother, who was an unconventional woman for her time. My great-great-grandmother lived well into her 80s, outlasting all three of her husbands. Lily's writings were replete with her grandmother's rhymes, poems and adages. The women in our family have been symbolically bound by the name Elizabeth, which we all share.

Illness dogged my grandmother from childhood, and she was frequently hospitalized. By the time I was five, she had undergone a series of throat operations. She was unable to talk while recuperating, so during my visits we scribbled notes to each other. I had just learned to write and felt quite the grown-up for participating in this form of communication; besides, it seemed only fair that if she could not talk, I too should be mute. We managed to form a solidarity between us. When I retrieved her diaries, I stumbled across those very notes.

In her later years, I watched my grandmother grow increasingly frustrated with her body and its refusal to cooperate with her. Still, she continued to push herself to live as full a life as physically possible. My grandfather would fuss and fret over her, and she told me once that if it had been up to him, she would have been "wrapped up in cotton wool." But she would often fire back at him that she was not one to *"sit on a cushion, sew a fine seam, and feast on strawberries, sugar and cream"* – a rhyme she had picked up as a wide-eyed schoolgirl who believed that life should be so ideal.

I was her only granddaughter, and I knew this conferred a special status. When I visited Northern Ireland, as I did most summers, I always stayed at Gran's house. She and my grandfather had very little money, but nevertheless she indulged me with thoughtful treats such as breakfast in bed each morning, long baths in her oversized tub and midnight concoctions of brandy with warm milk to ease my stomach cramps. As a child, I had sensitive skin, so Gran would wash all my clothes in mild soap flakes. Even years later when my skin toughened, she continued to wash with that special soap.

My grandmother's life was profoundly affected by both world wars and the civil war in Northern Ireland, which rages to this day. Her father fought in the First World War, leaving when her mother was pregnant with her, so little Lily was four years old before she laid eyes on him. He had been a prisoner of war; he had gone missing in action and was finally presumed dead. One day, he returned from the dead.

> *I do not know on what date he arrived home, but I can remember that it was evening, and the house was full of people there to greet him. Of course, he was being embraced by my mother and my brother and sister, and I must have been feeling a bit left out, so I pushed through the throng around him and said, "Do you not know me? I'm wee Lily!" I can still remember his answer: "Indeed I do, I would have known who you were if I had met you in Germany, you look just like your mum."*

Although the months following the family reunion were blissful, Lily's father was haunted by his painful memories as a prisoner of war. He developed a drinking problem and was chronically unemployed. Lily's mother cleaned homes to support the family, but she died of tuberculosis in her early 40s.

Gran grew resentful of her father, blaming him for her mother's premature death. When her father remarried two years later, she felt betrayed and did not speak to him for years. She even refused to invite him to her wedding. However, with the wisdom that comes with age and experience, Gran admitted she regretted the many years she had let pride and anger destroy her relationship with her father. I often recall her words when I am preparing a grudge of my own: Anger requires a great deal of energy to maintain.

> . . . *sit on a cushion, sew a fine seam,*
> *and feast on strawberries, sugar and cream . . .*

Gran's childhood dream was to win a scholarship to attend high school, and then possibly university. But when she was eight years of age, her mother threw this dream into eclipse with the stark reality that an education was out of the question. She would have to work instead.

> *I could leave school at 14 years old, and the few shillings a week which*
> *I earned would help balance our budget. Education in those days*
> *would not normally be considered important for a girl as it was taken*
> *for granted that you would marry quite young and then would be at*
> *home raising a family. I don't remember resenting this because, as I*
> *say, it was normal.*

Consequently, Gran had wanted to live out her dream of an education vicariously through my mother. This too was not to be, yet Gran's disappointment arose mainly from the opportunities she herself, rather than her daughter, had missed.

At 13, Lily began working full-time folding handkerchiefs in a factory. Her first day on the job, she walked through the front door and into the office to report for work. When she announced her name and purpose, she was told that she was never to come through the front door again. She was a factory labourer, and as such, she was to use the back door. My grandmother quietly left, tears of anger and humiliation welling up in her eyes. She vowed that her children would never suffer the same fate.

Perhaps this unpleasant incident sparked the development of her political ideals: my grandmother was a committed socialist. She campaigned during elections for the Northern Ireland Labour Party, distinguishing herself as one of the few Northern Irelanders who voted based on class principles rather than along dogmatic sectarian lines.

Electoral corruption was rampant in Northern Irish politics. In her predominantly Protestant neighbourhood, "loyal" Protestants would often visit close to election time to ensure that everyone understood how they were expected to vote and to "request" that constituents allow their votes to be cast by proxy. My grandmother made herself very unpopular not only by making it clear she would cast her own ballot, but also by challenging her visitors to explain what their revered politicians had ever done for the working people. She would often say that politics in Northern Ireland operated on "lots of fear and little support."

She was always frustrated that the working-class Catholics and Protestants of Northern Ireland could not – or would not – recognize that they had far more in common with each other than they did with the wealthy politicians whom they elected to represent them. Her dream of a united Catholic and Protestant working class in Northern Ireland never came to fruition in her lifetime.

. . . sit on a cushion, sew a fine seam,
and feast on strawberries, sugar and cream . . .

My grandmother idolized her mother, but her mother's religious prejudice triggered both confusion and hurt. Mixed messages of bigotry and tolerance were commonplace in Northern Irish families. Children were raised to believe religious differences should not pit them against one another, yet mixed marriages were considered unacceptable.

The intransigence of sectarian divisions in Northern Ireland was impressed upon Lily more than 40 years before the country's troubles intensified:

> *When I was about 15 years old, my sister went on a holiday to Enniskillen to visit a family who had relatives living near us. While she was there, Nell met a young man and the pair of them were attracted to one another. He asked if he could write to her and she*

agreed. Well! After the first letter arrived from Enniskillen, mum enquired from our neighbour if he was quite respectable before she would agree to a correspondence between Nell and him. She was horrified to be told that he was a Roman Catholic. I was shocked at how she reacted, as I always believed my parents to be completely without prejudice. We had been brought up to respect other folks' opinions, and since starting work I had many Roman Catholic friends. Nell was told if she became serious about Hugh, mum would never speak to her again. She declared that she had no desire for Roman Catholic grandchildren. There was almost a state of war; mum watched for the postman, and said she would confiscate the letters. I used to meet the postman on the way and ask if he had a letter for our house, and if it was one from Hugh I would hide it. When mum found out about my intercepting the postman she was cross with me. My sister became so fed up with the atmosphere at home that she wrote Hugh and ended the friendship. It never had time to develop into anything more.

My grandmother was very a devout Christian, but she did not impose her beliefs or moral views on others. Gran was steadfastly tied to Ireland. She sang songs of rebellion, was well-versed in Irish history, spoke some Gaelic and generally embraced Irish culture, all very unusual for a "good, loyal Protestant." I often suspected that my grandmother secretly wished for a United Ireland, free from British rule, but during those tumultuous times such desires were better left unspoken. She often referred to her religious affiliation as Church of Ireland rather than Protestant, which was exceptional in a country in which religious identity was so significant and narrowly defined. It seemed to be her means of extricating herself from the extremism plaguing both sides. Christianity was the foothold of her life. But religion was deeply personal to her, and she felt that exclusionary Christians weren't very Christian after all.

At 14, I confessed to her that I did not think I was a Christian. I expected her to be upset by my lack of piety, but she told me that

Christian faith got her through each day, and if I had something else to inspire me, that was okay too. What was most important to her was that I did indeed have that special something. I think she was conscious of the fact that although I did not feel a connection to Christianity, our visions of what constituted social justice were similar.

. . . sit on a cushion, sew a fine seam,
and feast on strawberries, sugar and cream . . .

Gran met her husband when she was 18. They married six years later. Because his family's veins were a darker shade of blue than her family's, and because a suitable mate had already been selected for him, my grandfather's parents would not endorse his choice of a wife. Unfortunately, though, all the unhappy in-laws had to live under one roof. This meant Lily's housekeeping, child-rearing and culinary abilities were under constant scrutiny.

After they learned of her father's alcoholism, my grandfather's parents often called Lily's morality into question. My grandmother never forgave her father for his drinking, but she hotly defended him to her in-laws during the course of many an argument. After 15 years of marriage, my grandparents finally climbed to the top of the public housing list and moved into a home of their own.

Lily was still folding handkerchiefs to help keep her family financially afloat. Each evening, she would bring home bales of fabric, ribbons and cardboard. Sitting at the dinner table, my grandmother would fold the hankies and pin them to pieces of card while my mother and her sister would tie the ribbons and pin them to the hankies. While the neighbourhood men would go off to a pub, my grandfather sat at the table with his family and cut the lengths of ribbon because he was the least skilled in handkerchief folding. It was imperative to Lily that her family spend quality time together every day and that her daughters grow up believing there was no such thing as "women's work."

Upon reading her autobiography, I was continually struck by the respect she had for the family. In Ireland, the term "family" extends beyond the nuclear connotation to embrace the community's value system. The extended family, most of whom lived close by or in the same house, were Gran's friends, confidantes and caretakers. My grandmother was the "glue" in our family. Her family always came first, a sentiment that has been passed down to my mother and me.

Gran died a few days after Christmas one year. My mother and I bought two clay angels, one as a keepsake for me and one to spirit my gran off to her next place. The angel destined to accompany my gran's spirit was hung on a pine tree facing westward, for the Celts believed that the journey of death is westward bound. It was an appropriate Irish tradition for a exceptional Irishwoman. I am confident my gran would have approved.

*I do not place my grandmother on a pedestal. Rather, I feel
closer to her because I have experienced her humanness, her
vulnerability and a part of her reality. For this, I honour her
with a memoir of the impact she has had on my life.*
— ERIKA WILLAERT

Sign of the Dragon

ERIKA WILLAERT

Railroad tracks
follow footsteps through
strange tongues of speech.

Armbands
blacken fleeting shadows of grace,
stumbling mightily.

Although I did not wish to wear the full-length veil, I could not bring myself to shorten it, because I remembered how surprised she had been when I first suggested the idea. It was just as well, for the dress could not be worn in the unbearable heat of a summer wedding. Instead, my mother made my bridal gown, and Po-Po, my grandmother, graciously folded her own away, playfully reminding me that it was, "the first Western gown to be worn by a Chinese woman in Toronto." My fiancé wondered if I should adhere to Chinese custom and wear the tradition-al *cheung sam* dress. I laughed, feeling far removed from any obligation to don the formal, tight-fitting outfit. I pictured myself squeezed into the slim red shell, my body encased in scarlet silk. "I couldn't get into it," I explained, meaning the tradition. He thought I meant the dress. I often have to console myself that we can't all be from Hong Kong.

Thinking back to a time before my own, I ponder the paradox of my grandmother conforming to the customary Chinese matchmaking requirements while deviating from the ornamental dress. I see her embracing one tradition that suited her heart, then skillfully rejecting the other in order to reflect her Canadian identity, the ideals to which she so strongly relates. The pride in her voice reveals her pleasure in having worn a Western-style gown, but the reverence she displays toward her parents' choosing a mate for her demonstrates her respect for her Eastern heritage. In this way, the paradox evolves from conflicting sentiments to a blend of two realities.

"THE CHINESE TOOK THE DRAGON AS A KINGLY EMBLEM AND THOUGHT OF IT AS A GOD"

"The first time I met your grandfather, I thought to myself, 'how hand-some he is,' and I was so happy my parents had found such a good match-maker." My grandmother's eyes, liquid in the light, always shine when she talks of my grandfather. "My husband was a very big part of my life. He still is; he always will be." She voices the words "my husband" with both pride and tenderness; as a child, I remember her calling him only Gung-Gung when she spoke of him. She often gazes up at his portrait, taken at her Order of Canada ceremony, and never fails to comment on how much the photograph pleases her. My grandfather stands poised in a three-piece suit, gazing at the camera with a warm smile, his chin held high. "Gung-Gung was so happy that day," she says. "I will always remember him that way."

I recall Gung-Gung better than I do my late father, partly because my grandfather is kept alive in my memory by the tales spun at the dinner table, as my aunts and uncles try to outdo each other in coming up with the most ridiculous of his shenanigans. They never tire of reminding my grandmother of how the two of them had unknowingly gone into the Haunted House at Disneyworld, where my grandfather nearly lost his teeth when he passed the mirror and saw a ghost sitting on his lap. They tease her about all the marked-down food items he would bring home from the supermarket. He would show off how many bananas he could get for 50¢, while his wife complained, wondering what they would do with 10 pounds of fruit. Po-Po wears a nostalgic smile on her face, only half-listening to the cacophony of laughter around her. She is accustomed to the harmless banter and understands this is how her family interacts. Beaming with pride, my aunt trumpets her mother's successes, asking rhetorically, "Do you know many people who have accomplished as much as my mother has with so few years of formal education?"

"DRAGON – A CREATURE WITH WINGS THAT CAN MAKE LONG, FLYING LEAPS"

Po-Po is extremely pleased that I have embarked on a teaching career. She probably regards my career choice as a continuation of what my father started before he fell ill. I know I like to think of it that way. My late father was a high school history teacher, whose passion for learning and educating young minds I fortunately have inherited. The graduation photos displayed on the wall of Po-Po's study indicate the importance she places on education. She used to remind my grandfather to ask me how I was faring in school, and he would ask the same question each time: "How did such a smart granddaughter come from such a stupid grandfather?" His humility would embarrass me because it left me speechless, but Po-Po would pat my hand gently and whisper how proud they were of my academic accomplishments.

"I got up to grade six," she once told me wistfully. "I caught up to my brother before I was taken out of school." At age 12 Po-Po had had to set aside her own education to help put her brothers through school. My aunt once told me that she thought the reason Po-Po had been so close to her own father was because he had recognized that she was special. He regretted taking her out of school, and as a result, tried to compensate by spending more time with her as a child.

"The most important thing that my father left with me was his love for people, especially family. He used to tell me, 'Jean, no matter what happens, your family is the most important thing. You may have friends, but you'll find that before anything else, it's your family that counts.'" My grandmother often shares these anecdotal wisps; wisdom handed down through the generations. I hear my mother voicing these same words, ensuring the message reaches not only my ears, but also my heart. It's difficult to imagine Po-Po's life before I was born, particularly as I know much of her work for the Chinese community was done when she was close to my present age.

"DRAGON: FIGURATIVE — A VERY STRICT AND WATCHFUL WOMAN"

Po-Po was born in Nanaimo, where she went to school until the family moved to Vancouver. "I was scared to death of our teacher. I'll always remember her, her hair in a tight bun at the back of her head. None of us spoke a word of English. We had to go to what they called an Indian School, and we had to walk past the other school to get to ours." Po-Po never mentioned the black armbands they wore during the Second World War, which distinguished them from the Japanese.

When I was younger, I recall being asked what I was and where I came from. I gaped at my interrogators, recognizing their intent to hurt me. However, I was immune to their ridiculous questioning. "I'm Canadian," I self-righteously replied. They laughed awkwardly, their balloon of superiority deflated more than they cared to admit. I never told my grandmother about the taunting. It was not worth mentioning. Later, in university, I remember how the representatives of the Chinese clubs used to harass me in the halls, insisting I take a membership flyer, babbling incomprehensibly in my face and, as I pushed past them, shaking their heads when they realized I had neither interest in nor comprehension of their cause. Eventually they left me alone, repelled by the cold stare I shot in their direction whenever they ventured my way. There is a strange comfort in quietly rejecting those with whom you are supposed to belong, but whose purpose is so completely incongruent with your own.

"THE DRAGON IS A FEROCIOUS BEAST KNOWN FOR ITS RAVENOUS APPETITE"

Po-Po has always encouraged adventurous eating. Sharing a meal is a spiritual activity that transcends social graces. In a restaurant she never orders from the menu. Instead, she calls the waiter to her table and writes in Chinese, with the required precision, instructions for preparing a regional dish in a particular way. I have imitated her particularities in placing an order, and as a result, food has become both a curse and a pleasure in my life. What was once cute – a pigtailed schoolgirl ordering escargot and oysters on a half shell – has become an indulgence of mine.

When Po-Po entertains, the guests sitting on either side of her (usually my sister and I) often eat more than they intend. Somehow, she always manages to covertly slip an extra helping onto the plates. Protesting without sounding rude or unappreciative has become quite the feat. Po-Po says grandchildren cannot be spoiled if they appreciate what they get. Over the years, my grandmother has never stopped feeding me the food she knows I most savour.

My love of food stems from my grandparents owning a restaurant in Toronto's Chinatown: Kwong Chow, or "the Kwong," as we fondly referred to it. Po-Po would take my hand and guide me into the kitchen to meet the cooks, who were stirring and chopping amid the rising steam. When no one was looking, Po-Po would slide a fortune cookie into my small hand. She and the waiters would talk and laugh together as I looked up, blinking, guessing at what they were saying. *"Doh jea,"* I would repeat, grinning and nodding as they patted my shoulder and looked down at the space between my teeth. When we were older, Po-Po taught my sister and me to fold napkins so that they would stand up like tiaras and to fold *won ton* so that the meat filling wouldn't ooze. The subtle gestures of hosting were never lost on us.

For family gatherings, the preparation of food is often done in assembly-line fashion, with Po-Po presiding over the stove, stirring and taste-testing the mysterious contents of each pot and dish. My family, following my grandmother's lead, uses food as a means of spending time together.

"ST. GEORGE FACING THE DRAGON"

My grandmother's career in community service officially began in 1957, when she was invited to Ottawa to lobby against the Exclusion Act, a law that prohibited the immigration to Canada of Chinese relatives of the men who had helped build the transcontinental railroad at the turn of the century. In the wake of her Ottawa visit, the Family Reunification Act was created, and my grandmother became the unofficial spokeswoman for the Chinese community. Her efforts were recognized in 1976 when she was awarded the Order of Canada, truly an honour to receive as a Canadian citizen, for her leadership in community service.

Occasionally she participates in citizenship ceremonies at City Hall. When asked to swear in new Canadians, she must recite the vows in both official languages. My aunts and I help her with the French pronunciation, and she giggles as she wraps her tongue around the foreign syllables. She thinks it is wonderful that we can speak languages other than English. Once, in Florida, when Po-Po wanted to speak to tourists from Quebec, she beckoned me over to the beach chairs, requesting that I act as interpreter. Even though it made me uncomfortable to be put on the spot, I recognized that my grandmother's intention, other than pride, was to demonstrate to me the value of being able to communicate with a broad spectrum of people from different places.

People often ask me if I regret not learning Cantonese. I grimace, remembering one uneventful year in Chinese school, and I point out that I speak both of my country's official languages instead. This is not so much a compensation as it is a substitute for whatever cultural experience I may appear to lack. I've been chided before, "Your grandmother can speak four languages. It's unfortunate you speak only two." I have never asked Po-Po if she regrets not teaching me to speak her mother tongue. If she does, it is one of the few regrets she carries with her. However, as she grows older, my anxiety over my inability to communicate in Chinese grows within me. I sense that one day, when she is gone, I will have the desire to find my way back to my roots, not as a pilgrim, but rather as an explorer. The intricate teachings of Eastern philosophy that were predominant in my upbringing lie dormant in my mind, waiting to blossom. I continue to strive for a time when I can weave these teachings and customs into my life. The seeds have indeed been sown.

"A DRAGON GUARDS ITS TREASURE OF PRECIOUS JEWELS AND RICHES"

The other day, I asked Po-Po if the importance she attached to "family" was a Chinese tradition. She is reluctant to distinguish Chinese traditions from those of any other culture – a family is a family. She holds my gaze with her own. "That's the most important part in my life, my family. That's why I won't show off what I've got, because I couldn't have done it without the support of my family and friends. If your family isn't with you, by your side, offering encouragement, you can't do anything, really."

I reflect back on a time not so long ago when I doubted my parents' decisions concerning family matters. In particular, I had many clashes with my dad, when my mother had first gotten remarried. I demanded an explanation for anything they asked of me. I resented having to wait around for Keira, my younger sister, or having to do chores and not receive a reward for them, as I observed my classmates' experiences and expectations. My objections would be silenced with the simple phrase,

"That's what being a part of this family is about." I began to learn that regardless of my trail of mistakes, my family would continue to see me as an integral part of their world. Despite occasional bouts of rebellion, they always inspired the best in me. My grandmother would remark on how fortunate I was that my mother had found such a special man to be my second father. She told me, without being condescending, that I would understand when I was older, and now, although I cannot always articulate it, I recognize how insightful she was.

People often notice how Po-Po and I resemble one another in a number of ways. We share the same round face, optimism and beliefs. I glance across the table at my cousin, who is explaining a magic trick to our grandmother. Meanwhile, she serves the last of the *cha-siu* to my dad, who welcomes the third helping. Since joining our family, he has learned, and added a few lessons of his own to our family album of values. Amid raucous laughter and storytelling at the table, Po-Po catches my eye and smiles back, mirroring my happiness. I want to tell my grandmother how I feel, right at this moment, but I know she already knows. That is what I love most about her.

Medal pierces pride
leaves a message inside.

Eager wings
chase unseen voices,
beckoning.

The process of writing this piece was unexpectedly stressful, mostly because I wanted to do justice to my grandmother. We all come from somewhere, and it is important to understand what that "somewhere" entails. Our grandmothers are certainly an integral part of that historical understanding.

⌐ EVA TIHANYI

Who I Am Because of Who She Was

EVA TIHANYI

My grandmother gave me shelter in the deepest sense of the word, a shelter far more than physical, far more than a roof over my head or clothes on my back or dinner on the table. She sheltered all that she loved in me and thereby ensured that it would grow. I continue to feel her influence in the directions I choose, in the relationships I cherish.

My most recent book is dedicated to her: "My grandmother, Elizabeth Kalán Tihanyi, without whom I would not have become who I am." Who I am is a dogma-hating feminist who insists on thinking for herself; a wife who has maintained her own idea of what it is to be a wife; a mother who loves her son unconditionally but has not sacrificed her own self to do so; a teacher who believes that a classroom is an exciting forum rather than a jail; a writer for whom writing is not just an act of putting words on paper but also a way of viewing the world.

My relationship with my grandmother spanned almost 39 years; it began on the day I was born, and ended on the day she died. The story begins in Budapest, Hungary, in 1956, the year of the aborted uprising against the communist regime. My parents, in their early 20s, were eager to escape the oppressive political climate and start a new life. I was just six months old in January 1957 when they crossed the border into Yugoslavia, hidden in a haycart. After much vacillation, they had decided it would be safer to leave me behind in the care of my father's parents. My grandmother and I were, fortunately, not strangers when my parents' choices threw us together. She had already been caring for me every day while my father worked and my mother completed her final university courses. The only difference now was that I would not be going home to my parents at night. My grandmother had become, in effect, my surrogate mother.

And what a nurturing mother she proved to be! My fondest childhood memories all celebrate her. The talented seamstress sewing, knitting, embroidering, crocheting – and finding time to put these talents into making clothes for my favourite doll. The two of us in summer, pitting cherries or shelling peas on the apartment balcony, enjoying the sun, the warmth of our shared company. The aroma of sugar-and-cinnamon–laden apple strudel permeating every room, my grandmother's cheeks flushed from the exertion of working the dough until it stretched, paper-thin, across the dining-room table. Strolling on fall afternoons to meet my grandfather on his way home from work, the chestnut vendor at his usual station, my delight as he handed me the paper cone, its heat warming my cold hands. Sneaking tomatoes in the pantry, biting into them as if they were apples, my grandmother laughing at my angelic countenance as the telltale juice trickled down my chin. And always the stories, the mesmerizing tales of princes and princesses traversing hills and dales, crossing countless oceans, outwitting foes, slaying dragons. Even today, when I hear the Hungarian version of "Once upon a time . . . " – *Hol volt, hol nem volt* (which translates literally as "sometimes there was, sometimes there wasn't") – I'm transported to my childhood kingdom, where chairs were horses and my paper crown gleamed gold.

When I hug my son, I am giving him the hug my grandmother gave me. When he curls up against me with an open book or entertains me with a silly pun, I'm reminded of my own young self snuggled against my grandmother.

My grandmother's nurturing went far beyond initiating my appreciation of fine food and literature-induced rapture. She was tirelessly exuberant, profoundly curious. Always an early riser, she had her housework completed before noon so she could spend the rest of the day doing whatever she wanted. Small things like the wind caressing her face on a spring morning or the odd shape of a particular tree or a sip of Tokaji Asszü, her favourite wine, would elicit a smile of pure pleasure. She would often stay up late to watch old movies – her favourite actors were Fred Astaire and Humphrey Bogart – or read well into the night. There wasn't a topic that didn't interest her. As she herself said, "Boredom is something I've never experienced."

Embarrassment did not come easily to her. If she felt like singing, she sang. If she felt like crying, she cried. And if she felt like swearing, she swore – as, she confided when I was old enough to receive such confidences, my grandfather had many an occasion to find out, firsthand. Embarrassment doesn't plague me too often either – though, admittedly, this is a state into which I've had to age. Like most people I was afraid of looking foolish – not just in others' eyes but in my own. I spent my first 25 years ignoring my grandmother's regular admonishment to "just get on with it" and quit worrying about what people did or didn't think. Eventually her attitude seeped in, and little by little I found myself releasing my personality – much to some people's chagrin – from the grip of prescribed correctness, political, sexual, literary or otherwise.

Age never bothered my grandmother; it was nothing more than a date on a birth certificate. She believed firmly that the soul was ageless, but was delightfully vain about the youthfulness this attitude seemed to give her. Even when she was well into her 70s, her voice sounded like that of a woman of no more than 40, and she boasted proudly on her 80th birthday that she had fewer wrinkles than some of those same 40 year olds!

She seemed fearless; I can remember nothing that ever intimidated her, and by her own admission, she would try anything once. (One of my favourite photographs is of her, helmeted, in trenchcoat and heels, ready to kick-start my grandfather's beloved motorcycle.) The future always held more interest for her than the past, though she honoured the past without sentimentalizing it. An enthusiastic fan of puzzles and numbers, music and books, her ears and eyes always open, she was culturally literate rather than intellectually trained. I often wondered what she would have become had she been born not in 1905 but 50 years later into *my* generation of women, a group for whom opportunity was more readily available. I found it interesting, and sadly ironic, that she had in her own youth fantasized about becoming a writer, and as a teenager would look forward to going to bed at night so she could lie awake imagining whole novels in which she starred as the heroic protagonist. Yet her support of my own early literary ambitions was never an attempt to live vicariously; my grandmother would never have settled for a second-hand life. She wanted me to succeed as a writer, not because she herself hadn't, but because she understood that it was what I most wanted to do. She helped me in every way she could – financially, emotionally, intellectually. Her faith was large and unconditional; I tried not to disappoint her.

My grandmother was, in today's vernacular, "a take-no-shit kind of woman," unapologetically wilful, emotionally resilient. Nothing could keep her down, at least not permanently. She was a person of conviction, of strong opinions clearly stated. She could argue the pants off you, but she did listen to what you had to say, and she could be – if you were convincing enough – convinced. Whenever I stand up for someone or something I value, when I let my opinion be known, I recognize her assertiveness.

Although when the occasion called for it she could be very serious, my grandmother was anything but sombre. Her sense of humour was irrepressible – she had a habit of sticking her tongue out at crucial conversational junctures like a naughty child – and she enjoyed teasing and being teased. She taught me early on that a life without laughter is a life not worth living. My friends adored her.

As I got older, she shared autobiographical details that made me marvel that she could still laugh at all. Immigrating to a new country is no easy experience for anyone, but for someone like my grandmother – who left Budapest shortly after her 58th birthday, one month after I had myself been re-united with my parents in Canada – it must have been especially difficult. She was leaving, literally, a lifetime behind – a lifetime that included two world wars as well as the '56 uprising. She had been forged in a crucible of destruction: starvation, bombing, pillage, threat of rape. She'd seen it all – and survived.

When she arrived in Canada, her English was limited to "please" and "thank you," "no" and "yes." Naturally, being the let's-get-on-with-it type of person she was, she enrolled immediately in English as a second language classes – which she took while, with my grandfather, she shouldered complete responsibility for running our household, which now included my mother and father, both working full-time, my brother and, several years later, my sister.

Never a whiner, her keen inquisitiveness and no-nonsense approach pulled her headfirst into her new life. Without ever renouncing her Hungarian roots, she branched into this life, embracing her latest home with respect and gratitude. Ever adaptable, she was far more open to change than my parents seemed to be. She showed me that you could embrace your heritage and your potential, but stand with both feet in the present while you did so. As a result, I have been able to avoid the "split allegiance" syndrome so common among children of immigrant parents. I'm interested in my Hungarian background, its culture and history, but when asked my nationality, I unhesitatingly reply, "Canadian."

Perhaps one of the most telling and significant events in my relationship with my grandmother occurred when I, at 20, told her that I felt it was time for me to strike out on my own. I had been living with her – by then she was a widow – for the past four years and going to school. A part of me, I recall, was hesitant about breaking the news of my impending independence. I didn't want to hurt her, but I was growing up. As I explained all this at the kitchen table over coffee, she listened and smiled. "You're right," she said. "It's time for you to stand on your own two feet." There was understanding, not argument. Within six months, she was comfortably settled in a seniors' apartment building two blocks away and forming what was to become a close friendship with her neighbour across the hall.

My grandmother was a feminist who didn't know the word. She lived out feminist attitudes, not because she subscribed to any given dogma but because they were hers. She didn't judge women in relation to men at all. Being female was, to her, neither an advantage nor a liability.

Always an adventure would have been a perfect motto for her. I strive to view my own life with such unfettered optimism, to accept change with such unalloyed grace. It is with this striving that she has most profoundly gifted me.

Anglo-Saxon traditions are recognized as quintessentially Canadian. I hope this collection will bring an increased acceptance and respect for the richness that "other" can bring to shaping our Canadian identity.

— ALANNA F. BONDAR

Seeing through Amber Coloured Glasses

ALANNA F. BONDAR

Here, landscape becomes my earliest understanding. *Before words, my thoughts drift to granite cliffs, mother to my poetry. The language of instinct. Perhaps then it speaks of my heritage. Beyond metaphor, these are my roots, now delving deeper than white pine roots dug nail scratch and toe into a wishfully dissolving internal crust. These are my veins, a crystal-lized quartz running white through grey, stripe to this landscape and hidden in beached Lake Superior agates. Deeper than jack pine's hold on remote cliffs, I hang to these edges like a baby to her feeding mother. It's this rock that I sink my heart into – though lacking soil-nutrients, it is a rock more solid than my ancestral heritage, forgotten in family photo-albums, black and white sternness and picture-posing clasped hands. Beyond stories that stopped being told as each member dropped mysteriously to famine in the Ukraine. Second-hand stories more twisted than my jack-pine frontier, more remote. They speak of a Stalinist famine, sealed borders. Zero tolerance. Youngest of seven sisters, my grandmother Rosalia receives a letter begging her to stop her generosity; the used clothes are too expensive a tariff. Another letter, scribbled in black ink, the hand of the Ukraine's intelligence explains the choking regime, their country full of secrets, the robbing of souls. In the hands of a Communist living in Canada, where my Ukrainian-Canadian grandfather has placed it, this letter pleads for recognition of a political demise. Instead, the return address is memorized. Word is sent to Russian Communists and family letters start a new cycle of hardly decipherable codes sent from Siberia. "This change of climate," the letter explains is "for our health." More solid is this new land I've been born into that crushes past hardships. Erosion moves slowly, as slowly as the thought that lost possibilities of the past could have made my Canadian present as inaccessible as Lake Superior's depths.*

With this prose poem, my thoughts turn to my maternal grandmother who – unlike my father's family, suffering nearly a century with too many hardships – struggled for a place of liberation. I associate familial whispers of pain and loss with paternal origins: wails of gypsy tunes played out on the piano in minor keys – always in minor keys – and the sad sounds of my concert-violinist uncle, playing from the rooftop in the old neighbourhood for everyone to hear. A free concert, inspired by melancholy that didn't stem from leaving the U.S.S.R., from missing their home village, or from remembering my granddad's home near the Baltic Sea, but from a loss of pride, knowing as immigrants they'd always be struggling to catch up. We are Ukrainian. We speak the language. We are told not to speak it at school. Assimilation. We must strive to be like others.

Pranciska (Eichas) Vasiliunas, my mother's mother, had wanted a better life for her family too; but her desire stemmed from her ambitious heart. Born the youngest of 11 children in a small village – Sakaline

Taurage, in Lithuania – Grandma was the only member of her family to emigrate here in 1929, to begin a better life for herself. She was following the promise of greatness and opportunity, but her struggle was long. She scrubbed floors daily, earning herself a hernia and thus cut-off pay. When she could, she would buy meat, confessing to her priest for having done so. Later she would say enough Hail Marys to absolve her of murder. Tired of waiting for the love of her life to be ready for marriage, she accepted a proposal from a rich Lithuanian coal miner in Flin Flon, Manitoba. Granddad was told he would never get a wife with his looks – even hair permed, expensive suit and all. Little did he know Grandma would have married the Hunchback of Notre Dame if he'd promised to feed her. Grandad married "the prettiest woman in Winnipeg."

My grandmother seems to rebel against assimilation. I ask her about the Depression years, and she lapses into a Lithuanian mumble – the stories lost to foreign rhythms. I lose the stories just as easily, without a translator to help me preserve them. I understand her in fragments. It takes too long to ask her about words I do not know. Slang mostly. People's names. She speaks of the old country. "Achhhh," she says, "old country . . . so many colours and dancing, always dancing, and singing. Oh how I loved to sing . . ." She sinks into a lullaby as she laughs.

She has not lost her mind. She laughs because these memorable snippets are part of the narrative. She can tell by the look on my face that this is not the way you tell a story over here. Instead, she tries to stick to the point, but the music always finds its way back into her speech as part of the telling. "Old country . . . oh, we were so poor, but so happy." Somehow it all seems silly to her, what I must think about all of this when my life here in Canada is so much better. Why would I be interested in these stories? She doesn't want to say much more – better I should have a blank slate, lest I be tainted by her poor past. But I want to know. I urge her. Determined to protect me from the recollections of the hardship, she will not budge, acting as though hearing the stories will make them a part of me. Despite her attempts to keep me from her past, I absorb her ways and pity myself at times for the traditions I have adopted, living in an

English majority.

Anglik – we all laugh when a "Brit-mix" date comes to pick up my sister. He says something foolish like, "I'll have her back by 10:30." No one listens. There are no borders here except the limitlessness of trust. We are necessarily "good girls." No questions are asked, but no questions need to be. *"Anglik – ohhh Anglik,"* my grandmother repeats to herself, shaking her head. Her discrimination against the "majority" breaks from the trend for us to assimilate. It's her attitudes that help me to maintain my individuality, despite my parents' effort to have us fit in, in a way they perhaps never felt they could. Raising us on the British upper-class model, my father forbade us to wear jeans, encouraging long woollen skirts and pretty classic sweaters. On Halloween he did what he could to protect us from standing out before we arrived at school: "I'll wait here – just in case nobody else is in costume." My grandmother somehow managed to counterbalance the fear of the first generation. She would respond, "Achhhh, . . ." and encourage me to dress as I pleased. Her encouragement was my sanity. I changed in the car to protect that spirit Grandma and I worked so hard to cultivate. In high school, I repressed the urge to break into song in the middle of a story, for fear it was not appropriate. Instead, I took voice lessons and prepared for conservatory exams, with my grandmother as the entire audience. Her smile guided me. "Always . . . you would sing. As a child, always singing. And such golden hair. Always . . . you would sing."

I am painted by my grandmother's naming of the world. Her words, her language, name things for me in ways that English fails to do. I did not hear her world outside the cozy cubical of her home, and it was like playing house every time I entered there as a child, like make-believe. There we developed our own secret code that extended the linguistic limitations. My friends, much too colourful for their mundane names, English names such as Sarah, Beth or Jan, were knighted in a secret ceremony by my grandmother, who designated names for them according to their personalities. Sarah became Schnek, a talker whose incessant verbal forays left my grandmother in a whirlwind, eyebrows creased as she strained to understand her. "She says nothing," my grandmother explained, "she is a talker." And Beth was quiet, much too gloomy for a child of her tranquil beauty; she was coined Meegla, an enveloping fog that rolls in quietly. Jan became Mahjzah, "a small bit" who never outgrew her petite stature. Later, when boyfriends turned up on the scene, my grandmother acted as the Oracle of Delphi. Her insights, my friends would say, were like hearing a code that had deeper meaning. I always suspected that her wisdom was actually her inability to retain English names: they were simply more words she was required to remember. She called Jan's first boyfriend Gylys. My grandmother and I both knew it meant "a sting," or a sharp pain, but Grandma told Jan it meant "nogoodnik." Despite the discrepancy in translation, Jan eventually stopped seeing him. There was no need for language disputes in a woman's world of untold wisdom.

But my grandmother's world was magical for more reasons than just her language and her quirky wisdom. She had answers for everything. Always thinking, always inventing a world of reason against the confusion of living without knowing much English in an English-speaking country. She was illiterate; she could not write to her own sisters without the help of a Lithuanian neighbour who, in exchange for a casserole, would write or read for her. Often her reasons made sense, such as the fact that her roses grew so well because she gave them coffee grinds and banana peels; that homemade chicken soup with cabbage cures colds; that if the grass is kept short, mice will stay out of the basement. But sometimes her reasons were simply odd. She would tell us that Sarah would never attract a good man because she read too much. It was not that being smart kept the boys away; reading actually changes the shape of your eyes, and in the end, it is the eyes that determine a perfect match. Her neighbour's husband had a heart attack because his wife didn't love him enough. Another friend's son was "slow" because he was conceived by a drunken husband. Then there were the explanations that would drive my mother insane in ways that she couldn't let go. They would spend hours arguing over so-called facts because my mother needed to believe that Grandma was all-knowing. For example, once Grandma got over her suspicion of light bulbs, she would not use any bulb of more than 60 watts for fear that the unnatural light would damage her skin. The microwave caused hair to fall out, phones caused brain cancer, and watermelon could not be eaten within two hours of going into the sun.

I consider the ironies of how I am now pursuing my Ph.D. in English literature. My academic work seems to flow with her vision of a new life here; I wrap myself with the words she continually reached for in translations. I immerse myself in the literature of an English culture, like a character in a children's book who has fallen into a keyhole. I do not slip into this world to alienate her or to run away; I am here *for* her, watching her live vicariously through me. Symbiosis. I continued in school at her urgings. "What do I do with a B.A., Grandma?" "Now what do I do with a Master's?" I tease her, asking, if she had her way, would I be in school forever? "Why can't you be like everyone else's grandmother and insist I settle down and get married?" We laugh together over the issue of my future, and she is proud.

I am my two grandmothers' namesakes; their forces continually battle between my first and last name. I am also a poet, whose training in the power of metaphor comes initially from the process of translation, with which my grandmother perpetually struggled. Empowered with language, I armour myself against the only limitations Grandma felt in transplanting herself into foreign soils.

While Grandma was teaching me her "facts of life," Mom was trying to erase the effect. She wanted me to assimilate into a culture that rolled its eyes at such nonsense. She wanted me to acquire a "Brit card," as though it were some club you could join rather than having to be born into it. So I learned how to set a table, complete with salad fork and dessert spoon; how to hold a teacup; how to talk to strangers in a way that made it sound as if the script were already written, taken from a novel. How to marry well. Grandma and I didn't need those boxes; she taught me that rules and etiquette exist for people who are too lazy to see each situation anew. Unlike my mother, I prefer my grandmother's interpretations.

When grandmother was near death, she kept her wits about her, though her veins, soft and blue, were bulging from her dripping skin, bruised with hospital needles. Her body, a skeleton covered by skin, held the active brain of a youthful woman. Born April 28, 1906, she was always a stubborn Taurus in every stitch of her character. When her health was failing, her conversations with my mother were in hushed tones, whispering things that would otherwise have caused her embarrassment. Visits to the hospital seemed more foreign to me than the secret language that passed between us. For the first time ever, she kept secrets: the need for a bedpan or a glass to be held to her lips so she could drink.

The day my grandmother died I inherited an amber pendant – given to my grandmother by her godmother. It is somehow symbolic of the real gifts she has given me. The amber radiates a vibrant smell of pine, like the smell of her perfume on the old scarves she used to wrap around her head. Her *joie de vivre* has no corresponding expression in Lithuanian. My grandmother would often balk at the limitations set in her simple country language. Her energy was so unlike the amber I wear around my neck. It speaks to my unique heritage.

Beyond clichés, I carry a piece of her with me, larger and more precious than any keepsake passed from generation to generation to be kept in what my mother calls a "hopeless" chest. Grandma's energy gives me strength. There is no need for translation. Her lessons contrast the pain I see in my father's family's eyes – that need to succeed – by complementing it with the true spirit of life. My grandmother would remind me fondly that, ultimately, to succeed is to learn first to love. I have been for many years so wrong about my heritage. I begrudge the lack of photos and diaries and huge family reunions. I wish there had been more.

Although I still believe that the Canadian landscape speaks a heritage that no other-scape can replace, I link my grandmother's veins, pulsing with blue blood, to the rivers of my destiny.

Nani ma was ahead of her time. Although she respected our cultural traditions, she encouraged us to think about the consequences of such traditions and how they would impact on us as women, as individuals. She reminded us of the freedom of choice. For that reason alone, I was close to Nani ma.

— DIMPLE RAJA

Pushpa: The Exquisite Flower

DIMPLE RAJA

To gaze at Nani ma, my grandmother, is to behold a flower in full bloom, captivating everyone with its beauty, grace and sweet essence. She is of a delicate stature, a petite woman barely over five feet tall. She manages a strong, steady stride, marked by enthusiasm and pride. Her hair, a silvery gray with ample touches of black, livens the memory of her youth. She is meticulous about her appearance, taking the time to make herself look dignified in her sari and matching sweater. Recently, she has taken to wearing trousers or long summer dresses, which also become her.

Nani ma has a medium-brown complexion, which I have inherited, and the softest skin I have ever known anyone to have. When she gracefully enters a room, she fills it with her vibrant energy. At parties, her vivaciousness and fondness for dancing always throw her into the spotlight. Her most striking feature by far is her dark-brown eyes, which bespeak compassion and wisdom, and also tend to reflect her oscillating moods.

My roots are in Gujarat, India, but my grandmother, Pushpa Limbani, was born in Zanzibar, a small town in Africa. For some 35 years, she lived in Africa and spoke fluent Swahili. Her way of life was much simpler then, but still she experienced many hardships. When she was very young, her father passed away, leaving behind a wife and four other children. Consequently, my great-grandmother and her five offspring toiled just to survive. Shortly after my grandmother was married at the age of 15, she had her first child. At 30, she gave birth to her last. She bore six sons and one daughter. My grandparents and their family moved around to various towns in search of work. To earn extra money, Nani ma took odd jobs such as sewing, babysitting and tutoring small groups of children.

In 1972, owing to political mayhem, my Nani ma and her family were uprooted from their home and immigrated to Canada. Three years later, my parents and older sister moved to Canada as well. I was born a year later, in 1976. According to Indian culture, names for newborns are usually chosen by the father's sister, and tradition further dictates that our names be selected from the Gita, our holy book, and then translated into English. (For example, my Nani ma's name, Pushpa, translated into English signifies *flower*.) However, since all of my aunts lived in Kenya at the time, my parents sidestepped tradition in my case and chose my name, Dimple, the meaning of which is self-explanatory.

As my sister and I were growing up, we spent an abundance of time with my grandparents. My father worked most of the day, while my mother was busy caring for her in-laws. Nani ma was overwhelmed by the move to such an intimidating country, and our lengthy visits failed to soothe her completely, though she was comforted that her immediate family was around to look after her and keep her company. A few years later, a terrible tragedy struck the family and drastically altered my grandmother's life: both my grandfather and uncle were killed in a car accident.

The sudden loss of her mate created an aching void in my Nani ma's heart, especially since her children were robbed of their father figure. Since my grandmother and I were very close and we lived nearby, the family resolved that I would stay with her. My time there sealed the special and intimate bond we would share for years to come.

Indeed, we spent many precious moments together. When I was young, I would lie down beside her with my head on her tummy and whisper to her in Gujarati, in which I had already become fluent, "See what God did. He took two people away from us at the same time! Why did He do that?" She would caress my head and compassionately reply, "It's okay, Dimple. God does everything for a reason." In retrospect, I believe I asked more out of confusion than rage. A child cannot fully understand the concept of death. However, in my adulthood, my Nani ma confessed that when I posed such philosophically grounded questions, she would wonder to herself, "What am I going to tell this innocent child? If she continues, I'll start crying right now." She always managed to keep her composure, though.

On a brighter note, though, Nani ma, a talented narrator who loves to embellish, would rave about an incident that frequently occurred when I was a toddler. My grandfather always enjoyed a beer after work, so before supper, he would eagerly pour his Carlsberg into a glass but would absent-mindedly leave it on the table. When my grandfather wasn't looking, I would help myself to half the glass! Then, feeling tipsy, I would dance around in my diaper and giggle out loud until I eventually fell into an uninterrupted, alcohol-induced sleep. Always, my grandfather would approach my Nani ma and ask rhetorically, with a giant grin on his face, "Who drank all my beer?"

Nani ma would reply, "Who else but your little monkey?" as he would affectionately call me.

Months after my grandfather passed away, I would constantly ask Nani ma if God would take good care of him and give him his beer every day. She would reassure me by saying, "Yes, of course. God knows what he likes and will keep him happy."

I consider Nani ma my personal educator. A significant part of my personality was shaped by her wisdom and extensive knowledge of life. She taught me a great deal about my culture and helped me discover the meaning behind its myriad ancient rituals and customs. I also picked up my native language from her, as well as other Indian dialects. Because of her lifelong teachings, I am now a self-confident and proud Canadian woman of Indian origin.

She brought me closer to our religion. All organized religions, on a fundamental level, are aimed at uniting their followers, since worshipping entails large gatherings and family reunions. To honour their gods, people fast and come together in harmony. Nani ma talked of the different gods; how each god has a particular day of worship dedicated to it and a dish to symbolize its significance to us. I fondly recall discussing the importance of our many Hindu gods with Nani ma and watching Indian movies with her that eloquently recounted their stories.

Among the many rituals and customs of the Hindu religion are those of the marriage ceremony, which can take up to five days. When one of my uncles and his fiancée decided to embrace their culture and plunge into five days of pre-marital ceremonies, Nani ma explained to me the relevance of each ceremony, and during them all, I was bubbling with questions. She became irritated and snapped, "Forget it! You just want to ask questions and not try to understand!" In Africa, Nani ma had not been permitted to pose questions about cultural ceremonies.

In accord with Indian tradition, Nani ma had taken care of her extended family when she resided in Africa. However, in this day and age, it is our immediate family that takes precedence, and though Nani ma and her ancestors had to follow the traditions of their husbands' culture and make their in-laws a top priority, she urged me to make my own choices as a woman and individual. While I am knowledgeable about my culture, I do not necessarily agree with every one of its facets. Nevertheless, I have the freedom to teach my children about their origins without imposing traditions on them.

Another of the many valuable lessons I have learned from Nani ma is that I can co-exist with others in this society by accepting myself as well as those around me. Growing up in the 1970s and 1980s, I was subjected to much racial stereotyping, and the colour of our skin often made my family and me victims of bigotry. I pushed myself to conform to the dominant culture and I craved acceptance from a society in which I felt alienated. As a woman of colour, I was – and still am – twice marginalized. If it weren't for my grandmother, perhaps I would eventually have come to resent my identity. She would emphatically tell me that if I took pride in myself, this sentiment would be contagious, and she advised me to ignore injurious comments from ignoramuses. Most significantly, she would proclaim that the colour of our skin doesn't make us any less valuable than other people: "Don't look at a person as black, white or brown and then decide if they are good people, but look inside their hearts and then accept them."

I was fortunate enough to actually witness how she stood up for her rights. It was then that I truly understood. When I was very young, Nani ma, my parents and uncles got into a fight with a gang of teenage boys. We were all walking happily along a Toronto street on Canada Day. One of my uncles, then a mere twelve years old, was waving his Canadian flag when the young thugs grabbed him, snatched his flag and viciously twisted his arm while shouting, "You stupid Pakee!" They ran off, laughing hysterically. My uncles, father and grandmother raced after them. My courageous grandmother pursued one of the offenders down the street, and then stood unflinching in front of the door of the apartment building he intended to make his refuge. Frightened, he hurled insults at her and attempted to push her out of his way, "Get out of my ____ way, old lady!" he screamed. My grandmother in return cursed, "No ____ way, you son of a bitch, not until police come!" He pushed her away again, but still she wouldn't budge. She pushed him right back and waited for the police to arrive.

Thereafter, upon hearing any racist remarks, mainly from schoolboys – such as "Hey, you, Pakee!" – I usually ignored them or told them to shut up as I quietly walked away. I was never physically harmed by racism, but this didn't compensate for the pain and anger I felt inside.

Nani ma always urged me to excel academically, using herself as an example of what a lack of education could engender. A victim of her times, Nani ma had to sacrifice her education in favour of familial obligations. She impressed upon me that while marriage and family are essential, education is something I can call my very own.

For 20 years, my Nani ma has nurtured and guided me. Even though she has raised seven children and many more grandchildren, she continues to place our needs above hers and to love us all unconditionally. At times, I still feel like the curious child who inundated her with questions. Without fail, I am filled with a sense of security whenever I feel her presence and remember her protective embrace.

In my eyes, she embodies wisdom, courage and maternal love. *Nani ma* is not merely another word for grandmother; my Nani ma is the exquisite flower that has withstood the test of time.

My hope is that this book will not only bring us a greater understanding of the differences that shape us as Canadians, but, more important, also highlight the similarities in human experience. We are joined by what we hold in common. In the end, it is essential to know and understand where that commonality lies.

— SUSAN EVANS SHAW

Twelve Golden Guineas

SUSAN EVANS SHAW

Immigrants from what has been called the "mother country" – England – never really experienced the ghettoization suffered by those from other countries. With any sort of British accent came a passport into society. Nevertheless, all immigrants were weighed down by a certain amount of emotional baggage, and my grandmother was no exception. Her need to impose the mores of a system she herself had abandoned made my relationship with her difficult and painful. Yet as a woman of courage and intelligence, she was my first mentor.

She was born Maud Jarrett on October 15, 1886, near Croydon, a nondescript suburb of London. Nana was the second child in a family of four daughters and a son. Her father, George Henry, was a contractor, and her mother, Lavinia Knight, was a country girl from Cornwall.

Photos of the period show Nana as tall and slim, with luminous dark eyes and abundant dark hair, worn in a loose knot at the nape of her neck. From childhood, her best friend was her first cousin, Janie.

Together, they invented a language, a variant of pig Latin called "Tut." Nana and Janie had used their language to exclude others in their stifling Victorian environment, and spoke it as they travelled about London on the omnibus, much to the disgust of xenophobic fellow passengers. She taught me the trick of Tut, and I in turn taught my best friend.

At age 25, Nana took her first and only position as a governess. However, at home her father kept a close watch on all his four daughters. To that end, he enforced a strict evening curfew of ten o'clock. Nana returned home one night after the prescribed hour and found the doors locked. My great-grandfather stood on guard and made certain no one went to the door as she knocked, frantic to be let in. She spent the night on the doorstep; a humiliation for which she never forgave him.

At the time of Nana's conflicts with her father, she had a suitor, a man who apparently loved her and honourably proposed marriage. Yet she refused him. Despite her rejection of him, her suitor presented her with twelve golden guineas. Twelve golden guineas – a considerable sum of money at the time – enabled Nana to buy a steamship ticket to Montreal. She packed her belongings and set out for the New World. The year was 1912.

Nana had intended to settle in Vancouver, but she needed to earn money, so Toronto was her first stop. From Union Station she – a naïve, apple-cheeked English girl with a training certificate and a single refer-ence as her only credentials – went directly to the offices of the school board. It took some persuasion on Nana's part, but in the end the school board official consented to a trial and placed her in a boys' school, where she was assigned the unruliest class. Nana ultimately tamed her students, though. She waited them out by sitting quietly at her desk until the boys tired of their disruptive sport, at which point she assumed control. However, her stay at the school was brief. When she heard there was a demand for teachers in Winnipeg, she headed westward.

In Manitoba, Nana was initially assigned to a one-room school in Warren, a village northwest of Winnipeg, where she boarded with a Metis family. In Warren, she met Stanley Peacock, the man she married and subsequently abandoned, staying with him barely long enough to conceive my mother. No explanation was ever offered for the failure of that marriage. Later I learned from a member of his family that my grandfather was an overbearing man, perhaps too much like Nana's own father. Stanley died when my mother was 17, and unfortunately she never met him. However, he left her his estate, which provided enough money for a university education.

In 1947, Nana retired as principal at Sir Sam Steele School. Her pension was meagre until sometime in the early '60s, when the Winnipeg School Board gave her a generous increase. She relished the irony of earning more on pension than she had as a teacher. She supported women's demands for equal pay for equal work; as a woman principal, she had earned less than the most junior of her male teachers.

I remember Nana and her coterie of women friends, most of whom were comfortable, conservative and well spoken. They met for tea in the afternoons, impeccably dressed (complete with hats and gloves) and coifed, so I naturally assumed that Nana had been born to privilege. In fact, my grandfather was, as the English put it, "in trade," although the family was comfortable enough.

Nana seemed educated, but I never heard much about her schooling, and I think she was mostly self-taught. While a young woman, she had done a stint as a pupil-teacher, and all her working life, she kept the certificate of qualification – her sole credential – hidden under her bedroom carpet for fear of losing it.

Although she was devoted to children, Nana disliked babies. In reality, she neglected her own infant daughter, and if Nana's friends hadn't intervened, my mother would not have been changed, fed and cuddled as babies need. Nana bonded only with children old enough to play games and respond to stories. In my first memory of Nana, I am perched on the arm of a fat, velvety chair, and she is reading from *Grey's Stories and Verse for Children*. I knew those stories by heart. She taught me to read almost as soon as I could talk, so I followed every page very closely. Nana told me years later that if she skipped a paragraph in an attempt to rest her voice, I would pipe, "Nana, you missed a part."

She retired before I was old enough for school, but paid a visit to my grade two class. She had just returned from England and, too impatient to wait, came to see me. Nana, along with my parents, burst into the classroom. She stood before us, looking like a duchess in her black Persian lamb coat and felt hat with a feather.

"Susan, come here," she beckoned. I obeyed the summons, rising from my desk to walk to the front of the class. "Kiss me!" She bent forward and I kissed her powdered cheek, too embarrassed to speak. When she released me, I returned to my desk, with all eyes focused on me. Nana, with the teacher's bemused consent, took over the class. Her modulated tones carried easily through the room as she posed questions. My classmates loved every minute and vied with one another to show off whatever knowledge they had amassed. Ten minutes later – an eternity for me – with apologies and thanks, Nana and my parents left as suddenly as they had arrived.

During the early years, my family lived in Sudbury. Whenever Nana visited us, I loved to rise early and snuggle with her in her fold-out bed in the dining-room. One icy morning in midwinter, a loud cracking sound broke the warm silence. "Look!" Nana pointed to the window. "Jack Frost has been here." I studied the frosted pane, awed by her power, aware she had access to knowledge I lacked. All the same, I knew Nana was not omnipotent. She never learned to cook anything except macaroni and cheese and never acquired much in the way of domestic skills.

But Nana kept my restless mind busy. After she retired, she lived in England with her youngest sister, Eve, and Eve's husband, Leonard, though she returned to Canada every two years. As soon as I could write, she began to press for letters. When I gained proficiency, I was happy to oblige. My letters grew longer as I got older, and her replies were always written on the folding blue airmail forms. Never did she print. I learned early to read her handwriting. For a time, to her delight, I wrote diary-style letters that I would stuff into an envelope for mailing every two weeks. One day, an unfinished letter vanished from my desk. Obsessed by the loss, I hunted everywhere for it, but to no avail. I subsequently ended my daily chronicle and broke contact with Nana.

For Christmas in my 14th year, I asked for a real diary, one of the five-year, locking kind. From January 1 I started making entries modelled after those of Anne Frank, a book I had read the summer before, despite Nana's inexplicable objections to my paperback edition. At the time, Nana had become a companion to a sick elderly woman in Toronto, and as a result, she visited us more frequently. Since she had never enjoyed much privacy in her parents' home, Nana had little concept of privacy herself. My sister and I felt violated as she read our letters, rifled through our dresser drawers, rummaged through our wastebaskets and perused our library books. I always kept my diary hidden under my mattress. Each night I settled back against my pillows and wrote by the light of a miniature reading lamp with my diary resting on my knees. One night when my parents were out, Nana came to my room to ask what I was up to. I had heard her quiet footsteps on the stairs as she approached, but her appearance in the doorway startled me. By then Nana was quite deaf, and because she seldom wore her hearing aid, we all made a practice of shouting for her to hear us.

"What are you doing?" she asked, peering at my lap.

Annoyed at being disturbed, I muttered, "None of your business," and put my hand over the page. With the unpredictability of the deaf, she had caught my words and she slapped my face. Shock, anger and remorse flitted through my mind as Nana turned and left. I heard the creak of the stairs. A hollow silence ensued.

Fear and guilt battled with my personal notion of justice, but in my heart, I knew I had to apologize. I found her sitting at the far corner of the chesterfield, looking quite dejected. Under the warm light from a nearby table lamp, her head was bowed and tears streaked her cheeks. I offered my apology, but it was extremely difficult to sound sincere because I had to shout to be heard.

"Never have I been spoken to like that!" she said, as she wrung a handkerchief in her lap.

I dropped to my knees at her feet, imploring, "Nana, I'm so sorry. I really didn't mean it." Then I, too, began to cry. Much later I went back to bed, but the incident still rankled.

My teenage years with Nana were extremely trying. Out of touch with the social changes taking place in England, she witnessed with horror my deviation from the "proper little English Miss" into which she had been desperately attempting to mould me. I experimented with fashion, hairstyles and makeup. Worst of all, I had an unsuitable boyfriend. She classified me as "common," a word that caused me to flinch. Yet I felt caught in the dilemma of trying both to please Nana and to conform to the social trends my friends followed.

By 1965 she had given up commuting every two years from England and settled here as companion to a widow and former society matron. The two of them, along with a live-in housekeeper, lived in a charming house in the oldest part of Oakville. On some afternoons, I accepted their invitation for tea and dressed as conservatively as possible, given that these were the notorious days of the miniskirt. I nibbled sandwiches and cake while we aired our oh-so-different-views on the state of the world. Nana tended to be sidelined by her deafness, but the animated discussions I had with Mrs. G. delighted her. Despite an underlying tension, they always invited me back.

Throughout my school years, Nana followed my progress closely. When I had to choose a university program, I disregarded Nana's advice to put my talents in English to use and instead registered in the sciences program. Studying English would have led only to a career in teaching, and I trembled at the thought of standing before a classroom of disruptive students! However, I twice failed to obtain a science degree, and the humiliation of that double failure was an emotional burden for years. To disguise my feelings of intellectual inadequacy, I strove in vain to turn myself into a polymath. The year after Nana died, I again returned to university, but this time I met with success. I earned a degree in French literature, a compromise that my subconscious had perhaps developed as the way to treat Nana's advice. At this epistemological point in my life, I fled from the world of science and entered the world of letters. Ironically, I realized how isolated I had become by incorporating Nana's intolerance into my own perspective and setting the same rigid standards for others as she had set for me. The

"In Adversity, Hold Your Head High and Your Shoulders Back"

KAREN DIAZ

You remind me of someone long ago,
She was the grandma, Elizabeth Battersby,
We now see you as the grandma,
You are the rock of the family,
Proud lady with white hair.

— VINCENT LEE CHONG, Mama's cousin, on the occasion of her 80th birthday

The more I worked on this story the more I realized that
Mama was a true feminist. She maintained traditional
family values and still worked toward change. I have come
to realize that I can be a mother, educator, wife, feminist –
each identity not exclusive of the other but impacting on each
other and on my development as a woman.

⌐ KAREN DIAZ

They call her Mama, Agatha, Mrs. K, Mommy, Mom, AK, Mrs. Kernahan, Auntie. Each of theses names describes the woman I call Mama.

As I sit here reminiscing on 84 years of living, I look back with joy and pride and loving thoughts on my family. My name is Emelda Agatha Kernahan. I want to let you know how I have felt all these years.

I was born on October 12, 1913. I was told that my birth took place on a Sunday morning at 9:45 a.m., just after morning mass. The midwife that was to bring me into this world was a faithful Roman Catholic. On her way home from church, she passed by my parents' home. What she did not know was that my maternal grandmother would be at the door waiting for her. Her plans for her breakfast changed – she would bring a baby girl into this world. My parents thanked her, and she lived long enough for me to thank her too. It so happened she was chosen to be my godmother and lived to pierce my ears and put my first pair of gold earrings in. I was eight years old then.

I was born in Trinidad, West Indies, also called the land of the humming bird. Our population is a little over one million. My home rested in the countryside, where the sugar-cane factories, cocoa plantations, coffee and the pitch lake are. It was not a rich country when I was growin' up, but we were not poor. We had all the necessities to make a happy home. As I grew older, I went to the school nearest my home called New Grant EC school. I stayed there until I completed the eighth grade. From there I went to a commercial school where I learned Pitman's shorthand, typing and English. I was confirmed, sang in the church choir and married at the age of 19.

I was blessed with two wonderful daughters, Marjorie and Myrna. My husband, Hamil Kernahan, died when I was 49 years old. At the time of his passing, my daughters were married and lived in Montreal with their husbands, who were attending university. My daughter Madge left me with three granddaughters to raise. After 18 months, I packed up my grandchildren and moved to Montreal. My younger daughter, Myrna, also had three girls, which I helped to tend to. When my daughters' husbands graduated from university and I was assured that they could all manage without me, I went to work. My first job was at the Montreal General Hospital as a nurse's aide, which I resigned from when I left for New York to pursue a course in practical nursing and earn a certificate. I returned to Montreal and worked in hospitals, nursing homes and privately.

My last job was a few weeks after I turned 65. I went home to Trinidad for a while, but returned a few years later and settled down with my daughter Madge and her three children.

My grandmother has given me strength when I felt that I had no more to give. She has been a friend, a soul mate. Her inspiration and compassion enabled me to pursue graduate work, raise two sons, be a wife and work full-time. I am the eldest of Mama's six granddaughters.

As she sits in the corner of her bedroom, with the sunlight spilling its rays on her golden-brown face and silver hair, she smiles a beautiful smile that radiates the peace that is within her. She is indulging in one of her favourite pastimes, watching the soaps. The television has been her companion for the last few years. At 4:30 p.m. she takes a break to prepare supper. Lucky is the person who happens to walk through the door at this time of the day. If it is not the aromas of West Indian home cooking, it is Mama's insistence that will bring you to the table to share a meal and a story with her. After dinner, Mama returns to her high-back chair, puts her feet up on her pouf and gets settled in to watch the evening news.

Mama follows attentively as the political developments of the day unfold on the television screen. Mandela, Bouchard, Parizeau, Chrétien, Trudeau, Clinton. Mama is a woman that understands politics like no one else. She talks about politicians and their respective issues with incredible familiarity. This knowledge and awareness stem from her life in Trinidad and Tobago when Dr. Eric Williams was prime minister. Eric Williams, an island scholar who had studied at Oxford and taught at Howard University, had worked with the Caribbean Commission to organize and advance party politics in Trinidad and Tobago. Through lectures, Dr. Williams informed people about the political system of the time.

One day Mama read about him in a local newspaper. Williams's vision for a reformed Caribbean and a changed country appealed to her: an independent country that would chart its own future, where men and women would collectively control and direct their nation. Mama always believed in change, especially if it meant the "uplifting" of people of colour, as Mama would say. In order to participate, Mama soon joined The People's National Movement (PNM) party, which was working toward acquiring independence. She was one of a few women to attend meetings and become actively involved in political initiatives. Political activism was unconventional for women in the Islands at that time.

"I wanted to be a part of the exciting change that was going to affect my country, regardless that some men felt I should not be there," she states unapologetically. "Women must have a voice and not accept the foolishness that we have different abilities than men."

To this day, her political interests flourish. Whenever there is an upcoming election, each member of the family can rest assured of receiving a call from Mama highlighting the issues and the importance of voting. After Mama had been living in Canada a while, Pierre Trudeau replaced Dr. Williams as her most respected politician. However, her political interests don't stop at the Canadian border. She can tell you about what is unfolding in Europe, Africa and the United States. "Knowledge gives you power and the ability to discuss issues which can influence your life," she often reminds me.

After the evening news, Mama takes time to call her family members and comment on the events of the day. My grandmother has always shown a genuine interest in all of our lives, especially when it comes to school. "Education first. Marriage second. The only way to better yourselves and to gain freedom is to get an education."

My sisters and I have heard this voice of reason throughout our lives. To strengthen her convictions, Mama promised she would pay the first year of tuition fees for any grandchild who pursued university studies. Her determination and support have provided us with a vision. Two of the granddaughters are pursuing doctoral degrees, one is a lawyer, two are trained in the field of telecommunications and one is studying to become a journalist.

"You must first know who you are, and be proud of yourselves as Black women, wives, mothers and friends. In educating yourselves, stand up for your convictions and make the necessary choices to pursue your goals." With a daring spirit she adds, "Do not lose yourselves in the traditional identity of what it means to be a woman, being at home, taking care of family." She has always emphasized how proud she is of her granddaughters' successes, and has insisted that we support one another. "Don't be jealous of each other. Be happy for each other. Each one of you is different, with different life situations. Set your goals and slowly work toward them. Don't give up. You'll arrive there, bit by bit. Don't give up." Her unyielding support has made us who we are today.

Mama's belief in the importance of education stems from the time when she was raising her own children. While neighbours and friends were sending their children to the local school, she was determined to give her two daughters the best education she could afford. At that time in Trinidad, convents operated by the Irish Catholic nuns offered quality education. One day, Mama decided she would take it upon herself to speak to Mother Philomena, who ran St. Joseph's Convent. Papa, our grandfather, was not in agreement with his wife. Not only would the financial constraints be difficult for the family, but, more important, he also feared rejection due to skin colour. Papa believed that as a struggling Black family making do, it was their place in society to send their children to the free local school.

Mama saw it otherwise. "One day I decided that my children were going to go to St. Joseph's Convent. I got all dressed up in one of the two linen dresses I owned, combed my hair and marched off to the school. I walked into Mother Philomena's office with my head held high and shoulders back."

Mother Philomena accepted my mother and my aunt into the convent. The first monthly payments came from the sale of Mama's gold bracelets. "My children and their education come first. I want them to be equipped to seek good jobs."

I am reminded of this story whenever I face obstacles. "In adversity, hold your head high and your shoulders back. It'll be fine. Be patient."

Mama's perseverance and family values have influenced our lives as women, wives and mothers. From the moment we were born, Mama played an integral role in our lives. When I was born, the custom in Trinidad was to have the mother and child return to the parents' home so that the baby and the mother could be well taken care of. My grandparents felt that my parents were too young to take on the responsibility of a child alone so they insisted that my mother and I live with them for a while. Raising a child was the responsibility of not only the parents, but also of each member of the family and the community at large. It was only while living in Canada that I was confronted with such terms as nuclear family and extended family. In the West Indies there is no distinction. All the members of our community were family.

In 1961 my Aunt Myrna got married in Montreal. Since it was not possible to have the entire family travel to attend the wedding, Mama went alone. While in Montreal, she heard about Sir George William University. She came across a brochure and brought it back for my father. It was her belief that if he wanted to make something of himself, he would need to go away to school. A year later, my parents moved to Canada, leaving their two young children with Mama. Mama and Papa took on the responsibility of raising us. A few months after our parents' departure, our grandfather passed away. Despite the financial hardships, Mama kept her commitment to my parents to care for us as best she could. She wanted her son-in-law to be well educated, obtain a good job and provide financial security for his family.

Mama believes that her spiritual connection with God will provide for her and show her the way. "Once you pray and believe in God, He will do what He feels is good for you and see you through good and bad times.

"Before he died, Papa had started to build a house for me. After his death, I was unsure as to whether I should continue to build the house, move in with my grandchildren or stay where I was living. So I prayed to God to show me the way. One night in a dream, your grandfather came to me and gently took my hand and led me to the unfinished house." She knew then that she should finish building the house.

At 84 years of age, Mama shows no sign of slowing down. The batch of crossword-puzzle books in the living room is an indication that she keeps busy enough. She is as sharp as ever. You can be sure to receive advice on everything from cooking West Indian food to child rearing, pursuing doctoral work or building a house.

She has taught me to respect my judgement, exercise patience, be genuine and honest. My husband and children love her for everything she represents in my life.

Every day Mama phones my sons, asks about school and asks them when they're coming over for Jell-O. They can pick the flavour if they tell her a story about school.

I have not regretted my 34 years in this country. But at 84 years of age and with a little arthritis, it is difficult for me to get around. I live alone and am happy that I have all the amenities. I pray a lot, and I know that the heavenly Father hears me. I am looking forward to living the rest of my days in peace and comfort, and to attending the university graduation of my great-granddaughter.

I thank God for my family and a happy long life.

continued from 131

world of letters thawed that rigidity and opened me to new experiences.

As I was trying to cope with the trials and tribulations of higher learning, Nana became ill with shingles. She convalesced in my parents' home, but when Mrs. G. died suddenly, Nana, now in her 80s, found herself homeless. Her once imposing figure was bent and emaciated; her hair, still sporting pins, was grey and lifeless. "You look like a refugee from the Salvation Army!" I teased her, annoyed with her slovenly dress, which on me would surely have been deemed unacceptable. Without a word, she left and slowly climbed the stairs to her room, and it dawned on me that she had suffered a great loss – her independence. Later I joined with her in her anger when her care became too much of an encumbrance for my mother. My parents finally placed her in a nursing home, where she died in 1972.

In Canada, Nana carried her pride as an Englishwoman wherever she went. Her poise and intelligence ensured her welcome. From the notion of being English, I too shared the pride, but I secretly lacked the matching confidence.

A visit to England opened my eyes and helped me come to terms with my identity. As much as I was Nana's granddaughter, I couldn't escape my foreignness. All my English books, clothes and training never endowed me with the qualities I thought I should have possessed. I understood the dilemma that had faced Nana, that of being a woman and a foreigner. She lived in two countries but belonged to neither. She and her sisters had, through their countless endeavours, managed to "better" themselves, but had lost the security of their natural birthplace and social settings. Her sense of alienation was first projected onto my mother and then onto us, her grandchildren. After her death, I came to accept myself as a product of the country where I had been born and raised, and my anger at Nana's misconceptions about our so-called "English superiority" subsided.

By 1972, I had settled in Hamilton and visited Nana only once during her final weeks in the nursing home. "Look at those people!" she said, her voice still carrying clearly. We were sitting in a sun porch overlooking a beautiful garden. "They're all so old!" Surrounding us were elderly men and

This story is an expression of my love for my grandmother.

JO-ANNE BERMAN

women sitting hunched over their laps, oblivious to the magnificent view. I cringed at her rudeness, and then smiled as Nana pulled herself erect in her chair to stare with hauteur over the room, indomitable to the end.

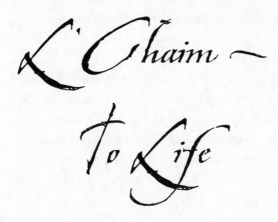

L'Chaim —
to Life

JO-ANNE BERMAN

I am sitting here with her on her bed, thinking of all our times together. Her feet are turning blue. They have become cold as ice. I rub and rub them, holding their life. Still they are cold.

An echo from the plastic mask fills the room. In and out, in and out . . .

The clock ticks its tock. As I rub her feet once again, I remember.

"No!"

"Yes!"

"No!"

"Yes!"

"No!" At that instant we both stopped talking. I stared into her eyes that were mine watered down. I knew at that moment she wouldn't give in, just as she knew I wouldn't subside. We fought with the same heart.

"I'm thirsty," she said. And I passed her a glass of water. We clinked glasses and toasted life.

"*L'Chaim*," we said in unison. We laughed, and then I said "jinx" because we had spoken at the same time and I didn't want bad luck.

Today her eyes are closed.

I am rubbing her legs now. So thin they are. And I look at the clock: 5:30 a.m. Bubie is an early riser. Soon she'll wake up from the pale blue sky of her hospital bed and have breakfast and smile at my aunts and uncles and me for being here. And she'll get up and spin the stories of her life into *babamysas* . . . and beg for the cigarette we won't give her . . . and wear the same outfit she wore yesterday . . . and talk about people . . .

"See her. See her." Bubie pointed her bony finger at the old lady in the wheelchair just three feet away from us.

"Shhhh, Bubie!" I motioned with my finger over my lips because she was three-quarters deaf – completely deaf when she didn't want to hear. My Uncle Murray, the hearing-aid specialist, had explained to me that she could hear only vowels unless I yelled into her ear. Sometimes it was easier not to talk.

"That woman, Sadie, I knew her since she was born." Bubie's voice boomed through the hall.

I wanted to hear the story. I could tell it would be a good one. But for politeness' sake, I motioned again with my finger in front of my lips. I knew Bubie would tell me the gossip, though. I could tell from the sparks that cackled from her eyes.

"Her last name was the same as mine: Steinberg. I used to be a Steinberg, you know. People would think she was one of my sisters. I had five of them and two brothers. Both dead now, and another brother buried in the old country before we came here." Bubie leaned closer to me before continuing. "When Sadie was 16 she wasn't married and she lay down on a haystack. She was ruined, you know." Bubie smirked, then peeked at me, before we both looked toward the old lady who sat crumpled in her wheelchair, her white shawl protecting her shoulders as she stared at the wall. Bubie smiled triumphantly. "She got married right after. Had to, after doing the *mitzvah* – except when she did it, it wasn't no *mitzvah*. Don't worry," Bubie waved her hand in the air and pointed to her temple. "She's *mishiginuh*. She don't know from nothin' now."

"Bubie, that means she knows something."

"Wha-a-t?"

A little louder: "That means she knows something!"

"Wha-a-at?!"

"Nothing."

I looked at my Bubie, and she looked at me, and we both laughed. I noticed that her mouth twisted up and to the left, just like mine.

Today her feet are cold and she won't wake. She can be so stubborn.

"Let's go downstairs for tea, Bubie. We'll get out of your room, and I'll do your nails."

To get out of her room at the old-age home, we would go downstairs to the coffee shop. In high spirits, we were ready for a jaunt. I would always order my tea with lemon instead of milk just to hear her say, "Some Jewish girl you are, drinking tea with lemon." I never did understand what the way you drank your tea had to with your religion, but I did know she was worried I would fall in love with a *shagitz* and not raise my kids in a Jewish home. To tease her I kept drinking my tea with lemon whenever I went to visit her.

Bubie frowned at my teacup, then she looked around the coffee shop and leaned in across the table to be closer to me, pointing her crooked finger. "You see that woman over there. The one with the grey hair?" she began.

I looked around me at the other tables. All the ladies had grey hair. I smiled and said, "Who, Sadie?" because I saw the lady named Sadie, huddled under her shawl, warming her hands around her teacup.

"She was ruined, you know," Bubie advised.

"Yes, I know. You told me," I answered wearily.

Bubie looked surprised, surprised and happy that I had remembered her words from before. She said, "Did you know she lived in her house with her parents and her sisters and brothers for the whole nine months and nobody even knew?"

"You mean she lived in the same house as her family and no one noticed that she was getting fatter?" I asked.

Bubie shook her head pensively and said, "To this day, I still can't understand it."

"What happened to the baby?"

"He became a professional bowler, but that's not the point." Bubie said impatiently, then continued with her story, "Sadie had been missing for three days when her mother searched the entire neighbourhood looking for her. She even came to our house. Everyone was worried sick, and the whole time Sadie was in the hospital having her baby."

"Really?"

Bubie sat silently for a minute, then said, "He wasn't Jewish, you know."

"So?"

"They got married in the hospital with no family around and then they moved to Cleveland, where his family lived."

"Was she happy in the end?"

"How happy could she be without a family. They disowned her and sat *shivah* for her. To them she was dead."

"Was his family nice to her?"

"Sadie turned to their ways. She didn't see her family again for 60 years, and by that time her mother was already dead – died of a broken heart."

"Just because she was pregnant before she got married or because her husband wasn't Jewish?" I asked.

"Family must stay together," Bubie said. "People don't always like Jews – that's why we left the old country with its Cossacks who burned our house. I was only four and my sister was a baby, but she started to walk on the ship on the way across, so we had to pay full fare for her. My father was a pharmacist in the old country, you know, and he had to start over here in Canada. He was a junk dealer here so he could feed us and keep us warm and dry. And even here people hated us because we were Jews."

I nodded my head, pretending to understand, even though nobody had ever teased me for being Jewish. The only thing other kids would say to me was, "Why don't you believe in Jesus? Jesus is Jewish like you."

"That's why the only thing I can spell is my name," Bubie continued.

The only things I had ever seen Bubie do were play solitaire, drink tea, and watch *The Guiding Light* and *Gunsmoke* on TV. She cooked cauldrons full of cabbage borscht and chicken soup when she came to visit us. I had never seen her read but I assumed it was because her eyesight was poor. "Didn't you go to school, Bubie? Didn't they have schools in the olden days?" I asked.

Then she told me, "I went to school until I was 10, then I got scarlet fever and lost all my hair. When I went back to school, I had to wear a hat and the boys teased me because they hated me for being a Jew. They tore my hat off and laughed at my bald head. I never went back to school after that."

Not being fond of school myself, and thinking she was particularly lucky not to have to go, I asked, "You mean your parents didn't force you to go?"

"My mother needed me at home anyway. I was the oldest girl in the family, so I stayed home and helped her take care of my sisters and brothers."

"Until you got married?"

"Until I got married. Then I had your aunties – Ruthie and Lily – and then I married your Zaidie and had the twins, your father and Uncle Murray."

"But what happened to your first husband?"

"I divorced him."

"Why did you get divorced?" I asked, surprised. My aunts had always been my aunts. Nobody had ever called them half-aunts.

"Because he was a bastard," Bubie answered.

"Why? What did he do?"

"He was a son-of-a-bitch." She set her mouth in a straight line, so I knew I'd never know. Then Bubie nodded her head. "I had no money but I took the train to Ottawa because you had to go to the capital in those days to get a divorce. When I came back to Toronto, the other women in the neighbourhood called me a whore."

"Why?"

"Because in those days, women didn't leave their husbands, no matter how badly their husbands treated them."

"But then you were happy for the rest of your life, right, Bubie?"

"I was never rich. During the Depression we were on relief. Your Zaidie drove a taxicab and he raised my daughters and our twins and even my mother lived with us.

"What happened to your father?"

"He died when I was 12." She shook her head sadly. "We were so poor that we couldn't afford a coffin for him, so his legs stuck out the end of the coffin."

I couldn't answer. I was too astonished.

"That's why I have money in the bank to pay for my funeral – just in case."

Bubie's hair is sticking up. I brush it because it's 6:30 a.m. now and I know she'll wake up soon. With all these relatives here I want her to look nice. I notice her fingernails. The bright-red nail polish needs a new coat. No subtle old-lady colours like pearly pink for her. She'll wear only scarlet. I get off the bed and walk to the bathroom to get her nail polish, nail-polish remover, nail file and scissors. I place them on the nightstand beside the vaseful of daisies and the telephone and sit on her bed again, gingerly. I don't want to wake her. She'll be up in another hour anyway. Later we can visit, and I'll fix her nails so she'll look nice.

"I'm gonna do Bubie's nails when she wakes up!" I explain to my aunts as they stare at me. "She tells me she feels better when her nails look nice!" I smile at them all, but they keep staring at me. I sit down on

I believe that narrative has the potential to move us toward shared understanding, in the hope that we can connect through our differences. When we are exposed to different ways of viewing reality, we expand our way of looking at the world. With this story I welcome you to my world.

⌐ GINA VALLE

the blue-sheeted sky that is her bed and rub her feet. They seem colder now and more blue, but I know it's my imagination – it's just the light of dawn playing tricks on me.

I brought my new boyfriend to the old-age home to meet my Bubie. I filed her nails and painted them red as he sat next to us. She smiled politely at him at first and wouldn't say much. I saw her sneaking looks at him when she thought we wouldn't notice.

"What's your name?" she said to him.

"Bubie, I told you his name is *Paul*," I teased.

"What's his last name?"

Paul answered, "Goldenberg."

Bubie smiled at him and laughed happily.

Every time we visited her after that, she flirted with my "nice Jewish boy."

She must be really tired. Her breathing is slow, shallow.

"You should get married soon. You're no spring chicken anymore," Bubie warned.

"People live together nowadays, Bubie, before they get married. Maybe I'll live with Paul and won't even get married," I teased.

"But what if you get pregnant?" she worried.

"They have something nowadays, Bubie, a pill you can take every day so you won't get pregnant."

She looked interested, but I could see that she couldn't fathom the concept. Knowing she wouldn't win the argument, she changed her tack and announced, "If you don't marry a Jewish boy, I will turn in my grave."

Tick, tock, tick, tock, tick . . . and the shallow waves reach the beach of the other shore.

And Bubie dies. And I am here when her feet turn blue. And she won't have to turn in her grave.

Homage to Nonna

GINA VALLE

Too often my days are packed with meetings, appointments, chores and tasks, and by the afternoon's end I'm fatigued and longing for respite. When I come home, however, I can rest assured of finding my grandmother seated on the cream-coloured, polyester loveseat that has been installed in my parents' recently renovated family room in their home of 22 years. There is comfort in knowing that I will find Nonna settled in her chair, unobtrusively waiting for another day to come to an end. Unless I speak to her she will say very little to me. We share much inside the home, but once I drive away in my Toyota, my grandmother no longer figures in my day. I learned when I was a "little Italian girl" in a predominantly upper middle-class, white-washed neighbourhood to close off my private life when I closed the door behind me and went to school.

My father, like many immigrants to Canada in the postwar era, faced continual hardship, maintaining three jobs, supporting a wife, several brothers and, as of 1962, a child. However, seven months after my welcomed arrival in this world, a pool of money was rounded up, and Luigina Valle, my grandmother, was sent an airline ticket by my father, her eldest son. By tradition and to demonstrate respect, when I was born I was endowed with my grandmother's name, Luigina. I, unlike many Italian Roman Catholic children, was not given a middle name either at birth or at the elaborate christening ritual. Whenever asked the reason for this, my parents have been unable to provide a suitable answer.

I have yet to understand the reason that my grandmother was uprooted and called to Canada. Were my parents in need of Nonna's help in raising their six-month-old daughter, or did my father feel that it was now time for him to be a parent to his parent? According to my grandmother, she had very little choice, since she was alone in Italy, and all her children were either married or dispersed throughout France and Canada searching for employment. She felt there was really no decision to be made. When the immigration papers arrived, she had a neighbour review the required documents. She then finalized the formal procedure simply by marking an X where her name should have been signed.

She arrived days before my baptismal ceremony. The black-and-white pictures indicate that I was an alert and happy infant as my grandmother held me in her arms. Little did she know that she would continue to hold me in her care for more than three decades. Each of her five children had left home by age 21; as I write this story I am age 33. My grandmother has spent more years nurturing my brother and I than she did her own children.

After raising five children with much hardship and misery, she went on to raise two more children, with less hardship and misery but with more supervision. My parents provided the money that supplied the food, the clothes and the home, but my grandmother provided the pasta dishes drenched in tomato sauce, the mended socks for our tiny feet and the neatly made beds for us to slip into at night.

My grandmother could not read the street signs or speak to anyone in English but each day she would bundle up my younger brother and walk up the street to fetch me from school. This memory was recently awakened in me while I was teaching a junior-kindergarten class. Many of the children were also picked up by grandmothers who could not speak English. The memory evokes feelings of comfort and security, as the reality did when I was a child.

For many years no one knew that my grandmother resided with us. "When I called last night an old woman who can't speak English answered the phone," some Jill or Kelly would drill me the next day at school, as only children can do without malice. "Oh yes," I would quickly respond, so as to not reveal that I was fibbing, "that must have been my grandmother. She was visiting last night." When so many friends had nannies and stay-at-home moms, I was reluctant to admit that I had neither of these status symbols, but a grandmother instead.

For 20 years of my life I resented my grandmother's presence in our home. Although she diligently cooked two meals a day for me, she was an inconvenience. Although she would handwash our delicate clothes and iron them the following day, she was an embarrassment on the phone as she would mumble something into the receiver and then briskly hang up with a clang.

On a series of Saturday nights that lasted for many years, I would often be found at nine o'clock in the evening ready to depart from home. As I'd make my final touchups before leaving for the contemporary dance palaces, my grandmother would turn to me and ask where I was going at such an hour. She would jokingly say, "You go out when the wolves are out. When are you coming home – when the rooster is ready to sing?" In frustration I would roll my eyes to indicate that her questions wasted my time. Without further acknowledging her, I would turn to my parents and inquire, "Why does she ask me such ridiculous questions? YOU, as my parents, don't ask such questions. Couldn't she just leave me alone?" I thought I made myself perfectly clear, and in less than a minute I was in my car, "blowing off" the intrusion. I knew she would not respond to my spiteful behaviour. It was an issue of power, for if I hurled an injurious comment at her, my grandmother would remain silent and with a blank stare turn her head the other way.

In the end, she had little authority over me or my life. She could not bribe me with money, for she had none. She could not entertain me with stimulating discussion, nor could she entice me by giving me glamorous clothes or the token gold necklace. What could she give that I would ever want? I needed to prove nothing to her.

I am ashamed now to imagine the pain I must have inflicted on my grandmother when I ignored her questions, cried out in a piercing voice if her comments were irritable and selectively excluded her from my life. I wish I could dismiss my behaviour as an extended turbulent adolescent stage, but I fear it goes further than that. I believe that the discord between my grandmother and me was rooted in my conflicted sense of dual identity and culture. It was only when I began to reconcile the two cultures in my life that I began to view my grandmother as an individual, a woman, a mother.

A change took place, but I cannot tell you what thought, experience or moment began the metamorphosis. I do not know if one day I thought about death and became frightened of losing her, but my consciousness did awaken. I began to observe my grandmother much as an artist scrutinizes the model waiting to be painted on canvas. I began to notice my grandmother's deep wrinkles and her sunken face late at night when she was without dentures. I would watch her as she positioned herself comfortably on the small sofa. Whether it be winter or summer, she carefully wraps a red-and-black blanket around her legs and feet. The television, which broadcasts in a language she does not understand, is then activated. As her day is without end, my grandmother can only hope that the noise box will either put her to sleep or help her pass the long hours, as one would do otherwise if a companion were available. I would watch her as she ran for the phone as if to make contact with the outside world, in the hope that this call might be for her, although it rarely is. Often at lunchtime she asks, "Are deep-fried potatoes and peppers okay?" So as not to disappoint her I go along with her idea. Within minutes the potatoes are sizzling on the stove, my grandmother standing over them, barely twitching as the oil splatters about.

My grandmother's birthday and Christmas are her two annual highlights. On the day of her birthday, in early October, she waits with composed anticipation for the guests to arrive and be fed, for the song to be sung and the cake to be served before she gleefully rips off the cumbersome wrapping paper and uncovers her gifts.

However, the winter months preceding the festive season are trying for my grandmother's mental and physical health. She inevitably becomes ill at least once. Talk of Christmas begins early with my grandmother, for she has little to look forward to now that both of her grandchildren are seldom at home. The celebration's procedure is similar to that of her birthday, with the focus once again on the gifts we have carefully selected for her. After Christmas, Easter arrives, with spring following soon after.

Living in someone else's home for 30 years has given my grandmother little opportunity to label anything her own, except for the cherished patch of land in the backyard that has become her garden. She begins her plans for it early in the spring. She nourishes the soil and watches over it each day, and is cognizant of the seeding and harvesting schedule because of her ability to read the seasonal indications of the land and the air. She is proud of her garden and enjoys boasting about the growth of each group of vegetables. To her great satisfaction, tomato salad is served throughout the month of August. In the fall, as the last of the garden tools are stowed in the garage, the cycle begins again as my grandmother's birthday quickly approaches.

Since my grandmother's arrival in Canada she has no longer lived according to her own rules. To a certain extent she has lived in a state of inertia since leaving behind her country of birth. Only rarely in her more than three decades here has she been called upon to state an opinion or partake in a conversation. As the years living in Canada started to outnumber the years spent living in Italy, older family members unfortunately began to converse much less in Italian. At customary lavish family dinners, my grandmother, with no knowledge of English, became a fixture at the table. As we impulsively conversed about what seemed to be pertinent issues, my grandmother could only fabricate her own version of the babble in English. Quietly she would eat as we were lost in obscure conversation. None of us seated around the table stepped out of our own comfort to engage her in our discourse. My grandmother has rarely asked for clarification on an issue. Some claim she does not want to inconvenience us; others insist she is simply not interested. People look past her when they speak, so she no longer waits for an explanation that never comes. When I urge my family members to speak to her or acknowledge her, they effortlessly respond, "She is so difficult to talk to. I never know what to say."

Did we, by our very behaviour, impose this silence on my grandmother? Or has she always been so serene? "I never became involved in the town gossip," my grandmother assures me. "I just worked on the land, and if there was extra food left once the children had eaten, I would walk to the market in Amantea and sell the rest. All I had time to do was to take care of the children."

In awe rather than disbelief, I insist, "But everyone in those small towns enjoys gossiping." I could remember only too well the stories that had been concocted about me when I had been there. Jokingly I go on to say, "I can't believe you didn't say a little something here or there."

She barely breaks into a smile as she responds, "Who had the time? We had to work so hard for everything. If you gossip, eventually you pay the price." To this day this stoic character refuses to participate in idle chatter concerning another's good or bad fortune.

When asked to recount her story, my grandmother, in her animated tales, speaks only of Italy. With sadness I realize that her life in Canada does not figure in her narrative. Here, the realm of her experience has been limited to the dimensions of our brick house.

In understanding only Italian in a sea of English and by being illiterate in a cosmopolitan culture, was my grandmother stripped of all mediums of communication, or are we to blame for not including her in our dialogue? Does our precious time not warrant the effort? We drive faster cars, take direct flights, use convenient bank machines and instantaneously access global information, yet we have less time on our hands. The very fact that my grandmother has been only a passenger and not a driver of a car, has taken a mere two flights in her lifetime, has never seen a bank-machine transaction card or gazed at a computer screen is reason enough to find the time to sit with her.

With few words of wisdom and even fewer of advice my grandmother has taught me more than any textbook or teacher ever has done. Whether it was expected of her because she is a woman or whether it is innate in her character, my grandmother gave unconditionally to my brother and I, expecting nothing in return. In our world of instant gratification, her capacity for giving is an admirable trait and one for which we would need to search far to find. From hardship, character is built. She fed her children before she ate herself. Undeniably, an act that many mothers would carry out, but my grandmother did so without resentment.

My grandmother's daily presence in my life reduced the degree of my assimilation. It is because of Nonna that I have not lost familiarity with my first language and culture, which I have come to accept as the cornerstone of my identity. The Italian language and culture connect me to my family, my childhood, my emotional roots. Language is the maintenance of culture, and because my Italian provincial dialect is used in the domestic domain, I have upheld my first culture and many of its corresponding traditions and values.

For many children of immigrants, Heritage Language Programs are the bridge to their parents' homeland. Nonna is the bridge in my life. My parents worked diligently to break out of the low socioeconomic condition into which they had stepped when they first arrived in Canada, and so there was little time available for them to reminisce about their homeland. Nonna and I to this day converse in the language that links me to my roots – my parents' and grandmother's native land.

While other children of immigrants attended Heritage Language Programs, Nonna became my heritage language program. The language I speak with her is the one lasting link between the first and second generation. With Nonna now in her 94th year, I often wonder how much longer she will be with us. I begin to question if I have the vision to stimulate a resurgence of interest in our first language and culture. If the language no longer remains an integral part of us, the culture will be reduced to a handful of static traditions and family gatherings. I fear that when Nonna will figure only spiritually in my life, the language and culture will dissolve. The bridge will dismantle, and what used to be an essential aspiration will never be attained.

My grandmother has no voice. When she speaks she is not heard. I am

*We sent my grandmother to heaven from a mosque on a cold
November day, several years after this story was written. The
garden of the mosque was filled with family and friends.
Afterwards, while walking with my aunt on the banks of the
Bosphorus near the apartment where my grandmother had
lived for more than 30 years, shopkeepers, fishermen
and friends of my grandmother stopped us to express their
condolences. Later that evening more relatives and family
friends came to another ceremony at my great-aunt's house.
Enormous quantities of tea and food were brought out, as
visitors continued to come to pay their last respects. Suddenly,
standing in the crowded parlour, numb from the shock of the
day's events, I understood what an impact she had had on the
lives of so many people.*

⌐ ZEYNEP VAROGLU

writing my grandmother's story because my voice is heard and my words will be read. Perhaps the meaning of her words will not be entirely unveiled in this manner, but by relaying her story the significance of her presence in my life is acknowledged.

This tribute to my grandmother is long overdue. Although the years of resentment cannot be washed away, engendering an appreciation for my first language and culture in those around me will remain a central focus in my life and not evaporate with the memories of Nonna.

Afternoon Tea in the Clouds

ZEYNEP VAROGLU

The bus from Paris to Istanbul passed through Italy and Greece and finally crossed the Turkish border into Edirne at about 2 a.m. – after four days and nights. By the time I arrived at my destination, I was exhausted and overwhelmed. I needed to energize myself to complete the last leg of the trip to my grandmother's apartment, and I managed to find a youth hostel in Sultan Ahmet, on the European side of the Bosphorus.

The innkeeper eyed me with suspicion. "This is the room. Here's the key. It's small but clean, nothing fancy. This is a cheap hotel, you know." He then muttered under his breath, "The bathroom and shower are down the hall. Don't worry about security. We don't let Turks stay here, only Americans and Europeans. You don't have to lock your door."

I wondered if he had caught the irony of his comments as I handed him my passport. I took a shower and scrubbed off the dust from my trip, returned to my room and lapsed into a sound slumber.

The call of the muezzin woke me as the afternoon sun burst into the room. It was time to cross over to the Asian side of Istanbul. As I prepared my bag for departure, I could hear tourists talking in chords of French, German and English. At the ferry terminal by the Bosphorus, men sold *simit* – fresh bread rings – while crowds rushed to catch the ferries criss-crossing between Asia and Europe. When I disembarked from the ferry in Kadikoy, some gypsy children tugged at my bag, taking me for a foreign backpacker. "Hello! Hello! Change? Change?" they repeated in broken English. Finally I responded in Turkish, "I haven't got anything for you!"

In the four years since my last visit, Istanbul had expanded to accommodate even more people. During the taxi ride to the suburbs – where my grandmother lived in her new apartment on the 12th floor of a high-rise – the horizon seemed to be closing in on the street. The taxi driver headed between Ataturk and Inonu Streets – named after the founder of the Turkish Republic and the first prime minister, respectively.

"You finally came!" my grandmother exclaimed. "We've been waiting for you. Look, your great-aunt Nurten is here too."

"Girl, how have you been? Aah, come in here and let me see you," Aunt Nurten beckoned from the parlour.

"She doesn't look as bad as last time, does she, Nurten?" my grandmother asked. "We've been waiting for you to come for so long. Nobody knew what had happened to you. We heard that you were passing through Paris and then we didn't hear anything more. How was your trip? Let's eat! I have some things ready in the fridge. Put your bag down. Oh, it looks so heavy. Did you carry that all by yourself?"

The first two days at my grandmother's, I was tired from the trip and could do little more than eat, sleep and watch television. My grandmother seemed pleased, though. While we watched commentaries on the morning news, we ate a breakfast consisting of fresh bread, cheese, olives, tea and hard-boiled eggs. I fell back asleep as my grandmother took to cleaning her apartment. A Turkish version of MTV entertained us during lunch. In the afternoon, I explored the apartment, the Turkish, English and French books and the photos. Tea was served at four o'clock and supper during the evening news two hours later. After supper, another political commentary; then, finally, something we could both agree on: Turkish movies dating back to the 1960s and 1970s, at nine o'clock. We sat on the couch together. I put my head on her lap, and she stretched her legs out onto the footstool, clutching the remote control. We were transported back to a time when our daily routine was different, and yet just the same.

On top of the TV, pictures of my grandfather, my aunt, my uncle, my mother and my grandmother's wedding stared back at us.

For years, my grandmother had only dreamed of moving up and into the clouds from her ground-floor flat on the European side of Istanbul. She had moved into this flat in the early '60s, accompanied by her three children: my mother and my mother's brother and sister. This was the home where I was brought to live after my mother died, when I was just 10 months old. My grandmother was the first woman I called mother.

When I lived with my grandmother on the ground floor, we had our routines. Each morning we would wash our faces together, then have breakfast while listening to the radio – a clunky wooden box we took turns kicking when it stopped working. My grandmother would say every morning after breakfast, "This apartment is too stuffy. There's no air. One day we'll move into an apartment on the top floor. We'll have a large window, and every morning we'll have air. This stuffy apartment is starting to give me a headache!" Then the radio would go on the fritz again, she would send me to kick it, and the conversation would turn to our plans for the day. Some days we would visit relatives or shop for groceries. On the streets, I would proudly hold my grandmother's hand. Storekeepers greeted us and asked about my aunt, or smiled at me while my grandmother shopped. On the way home, we would stop for tea in one of the tea shops near our flat.

We usually visited my grandmother's sisters or my great-grandmother and great-great-aunt. There was always family, which meant other women. Men did not exist in my world with my grandmother. The men who were around were inconsequential. Sometimes my great-aunts' husbands would come in momentarily, say hello and promptly disappear. My uncle would visit with us occasionally, but he was busy with his life in another city. It seemed that men vanished either due to death or other unfortunate circumstances – leaving my grandmother's world simpler and tidier. Women talked, cooked, fed and managed life. Men were but fragile ornaments.

Among my favourite women were my great-aunt Nurten and her daughters. As a three year old, I considered her daughters, my *ablas* (sisters), epitomes of sophistication. To my young eyes, all three adolescent *ablas* appeared mysterious. They smelled of powder makeup, wore soft satiny fabrics and moved to the rhythms of Turkish pop music, a mix of Middle Eastern ballads about lost love, set to the tune of the lute and the American electric guitar. I would follow my *ablas* around their apartment, attempting to sink as deep as I could into their world, hoping my admiration would be my guide. I was offered a taste of this glamorous world via my great-aunt's spread of sweet and savoury biscuits – and tea, which simmered in the afternoon sun flooding into the parlour.

Watching the news and Turkish-dubbed American sitcoms such as *The Fugitive* or *Bonanza* was almost a nightly ritual. I would always fall asleep on my grandmother's lap as she quietly lectured, "You must always be clean, polite, study hard and be *cici* (nice)." At the time, such instructions seemed obvious and simplistic. She never warned me I would one day have to leave the comfort of her lap forever.

The most influential men in our lives were found in three pictures on the mantelpiece. The first was a black-and-white photo of my grandfather in his naval-officer uniform. He died in the 1950s, leaving my grandmother with three young children, a cabinet full of books on deep-sea surgery and a small pension.

The second was a smudged photo of my father, which was shoved into the side of a frame containing a larger picture of the woman no one talked about. My father lived with my brother in Vancouver, Canada, which was more conveniently referred to as "America" and which my grandmother explained to me was just like where the people on *Bonanza* and *The Fugitive* lived. He wrote letters and sent me toys.

The third and largest picture was of the most revered man in Turkey, Ataturk. "Ataturk," my grandmother would enunciate, to ensure that I could fully understand, "brought great things to Turkey." My grandmother started school one year after Ataturk had proclaimed Turkey a republic. Ataturk had redefined the role of Turkish women when my grandmother was a young girl, declaring that women should be educated and occupy a position equal to that of men. My grandmother had learned to take these words literally when she found herself widowed with three small children to support.

Ironically, once my grandmother moved to her apartment in the sky, separated from the neighbours who had lived near her ground-floor flat, she spent more time with these photos than with actual people. The photos, constantly present, disappointed less than real people did. She rarely left her apartment. Her groceries were delivered to her door every day. She would often speak over the telephone to her friends, offering them advice. She cleaned the apartment daily and stored the cooked food meant for guests and me in two refrigerators.

When I was five my father and brother returned to Turkey. The day they were expected, we went onto the upstairs-neighbours' balcony to wait for them. There was a disturbing electricity in the air. The serenity and comfort of our world seemed in jeopardy. We finally noticed a man walking down the street with a small boy. My grandmother turned to me and said, "You remember your father and brother don't you?" I thought to myself, "Sure, I remember a photo."

My brother lived with us for a while. He was generally a gentle and good-natured playmate who just didn't seem to understand anything about afternoon tea, visiting relatives and speaking Turkish. In short, he was a stranger to life in my grandmother's ground-floor flat. Everything had to be spelled out and shown to him. Though he was older than me, I felt responsible for him. But he knew something I didn't. During one of our frequent squabbles, my brother revealed, "And another thing, you're so dumb you don't even know that Grandma is our grandma and that our mother's dead!" The fight came to an abrupt halt. I turned to my grandmother for confirmation, and she nodded. I went over to the mantelpiece and found the big picture of the woman no one talked about and asked my grandmother if this was my mother. Affirmative.

Soon after this particular visit, I moved to Ankara with my father and brother. My father remarried and I had a new "mother." Thereafter, I was often not permitted to stay with my grandmother. Under my father's roof, there were numerous rules by which to abide. Comfort was replaced by efficiency, and afternoon tea in the parlour by dinner around a table. That summer, my father allowed my visit with my grandmother and aunt to run a little longer than usual, but my grandmother was tense and quiet. We spent a lot of time shopping and taking pictures. It seemed that my grandmother was trying to prepare me for something while trying to preserve something else for herself. Several weeks after this trip to Istanbul, I moved to Canada.

I had been with my grandmother for three days and now felt claustrophobic in her apartment. The pictures on the mantelpiece, after all these years, appeared to be exploding from their frames. I had to escape! My great-aunt Nurten had come over for afternoon tea. "I'm going out. I'm going to Kadikoy. I'll see you later," I said.

"You're not going out looking like that, are you?" my grandmother asked.

"Yes, I am," I replied. "Is there something wrong with what I have on?"

"Well, your skirt looks old and it's not hanging very well in the front. Give it to me tonight, and I'll see what I can do. Why don't you wear your aunt's nice white outfit?"

"It's true, darling," my great-aunt Nurten whispered sweetly in my ear as I kissed her goodbye, "You really don't know how to dress!"

In Kadikoy the gypsy children ignored me, and the police nearly ran me over as I was crossing the street to get to the café next to the ferry docks. In spite of everything, after these few days with my grandmother,

I was no longer an outsider and foreigner but someone who belonged. I would escape detection as long as I didn't attempt to speak Turkish, which was now laced with an English accent.

I ordered tea and a cheese sandwich as I watched the sunset over the minarets of the Aya Sofia. I listened to the sounds of the ferries transporting people home after a day in the city, and I started to relax and breathe again. A Turkish newspaper, another cup of tea and the sun had set. This hustle and bustle was what I'd missed most since I'd left Turkey the first time.

It was the isolation and emptiness of life in Canada that had plagued me from the beginning. From my first wet fall in Vancouver, human relations appeared antiseptic. There were no smiling shopkeepers to wave at as I passed by. The cashier at the local Safeway seemed to revel in hollering at me whenever I touched any item. In school, my peers were totally incomprehensible, and family life was much more complicated than I had ever envisioned it. When we arrived in Canada, my brother and I changed roles: he seemed to be in his element while I felt off balance. My foundation was no longer what I had known it to be. I had lost my grandmother, and with her, my entire family of women, of cooking, visiting, socializing and circular endless time. Suddenly I had to learn to walk, talk, play and laugh all over again. Nothing was as it used to be. Everyone around me appeared to be acting erratically. Above all else, I felt empty in this sterile world.

At first, I tried to tell others of the life I had shared with my grandmother. In grade one, when the teacher asked us to talk about our families, I recounted stories about my *ablas,* great-aunts, aunt and, most significant, my grandmother. The teacher seemed disappointed and angry. Frustrated, she said that I was not doing the task. She meant my family: my mother, father, siblings. Was it a problem with my English that I just didn't understand such simple instructions? I learned that "family" didn't mean the same thing in Canada as it did in Turkey. In Canada families were much smaller and isolated – often dissected as clinically as mine had been in order to preserve the nucleus. In Turkey I had been taught that family included all the people it took to make a person a full member of a social group. It quickly became evident that sharing my reality, with its foreign language, afternoon teas, biscuits and soft satiny fabrics, had only made me strange to my classmates.

Survival now depended on adhering to a new code of conduct. I worked feverishly to conceal my past and memories from my teachers and other children who called this wet, cold place home. I became reserved. Sometimes my grandmother and aunt would call, and I would hear their voices from a world now so distant. I desperately wanted to escape, even for a moment, to my grandmother's flat on the ground floor, but at the same time, I was fearful of the effect that the invasion of these memories would have on my life in Canada.

When I visited friends whose grandparents lived nearby, I was often resentful of their good fortune. I looked for traces of my grandmother; a kind word or gesture – I would take anything. I sadly came to realize that my grandmother and her ground-floor flat could not be reconstructed in Vancouver. My Turkish grandmother could not fit into my Canadian world.

On the bus back to my grandmother's apartment, I felt a sense of urgency. When I entered the apartment, my grandmother was watching the news while cooking.

"Have you had dinner? I've made some vegetables especially for you. Here, set the table. Oh, don't change the channel, there's a very important documentary on the constitution coming up and I don't want to miss it.

"How is your brother?" she went on to ask. "Why doesn't he come visit anymore? Do you talk to him often? I called him last month, and he invited me to stay with him in his house in America. How come you never invite me to your house? You know it's been such a long time since the family last saw your brother," she concluded, as we set the table together, emptying the contents of the two fridges, which contained enough food for six and far too much for us two. I looked up to see the photo, taken on the Turkish seacoast, of my brother and me during a summer vacation 10 years earlier. My brother was 16 and I was 14. On this trip, my grandmother seemed older and her movements slower than usual. That summer, my brother and I were forced to spend a lot of time together. My brother found the pace and routine slow and tedious. I tried to explain the logic behind it, but I myself was beginning to forget. I had been living in Canada for nearly 10 years and had adapted to my new environment. We fussed over our grandmother, but I felt restless, and my brother even more so. For the first time, I began to understand why my grandmother always complained there was not enough ventilation in her ground-floor flat.

That same summer, my aunt took us to the Aegean coast. My brother left my grandmother, my aunt and me alone, opting for the underwater. He snorkelled away his nervousness, while I watched my aunt and grandmother closely, trying to make sense of myself as a person separate from them. I knew I was not like my father, but suddenly I suspected I might not resemble my grandmother or aunt either.

Upon my return to Canada, for the first time I did not long for Istanbul and the ground-floor flat. As I reflected on Turkey, I was finally at peace, accepting that a part of me had not been left behind there.

"Grandma," I interjected, "You know when I was in Kadikoy, I saw – "

"Hold on, I'm just going to change the channel. What do you think of this fabric? I've been saving it for a long time, I was going to make something for your mother when she got married, but never got a chance. I saved it, thinking maybe I could make you a dress one day. You know, all the young girls are wearing this pattern this year. Could you turn up the volume?"

"Yes, Grandma," I nodded, "I was saying that when I was in Kadikoy, I saw – "

"Uh-huh, yes, when are you going to your *abla*'s house? I think she invited you there this weekend, and then you have to go and visit your aunt and, of course, your uncle and his family. Let's see, did you put the rice on the table? I think there's something more in the fridge."

"Yes, Grandma, what I was saying was that I saw a book sale in

Kadikoy this afternoon, and I bought some – "

"You have to visit your uncle. They've been calling the last couple of days. He's very busy with his shop, but he wants you to go to their house. You can get the bus to Bursa over on Inonu street. He'll send one of the boys to meet you at the station. What were you saying?"

"Nothing," I responded, "I'll go tomorrow to Bursa, Grandma."

Several days later, I sat in my uncle's small café. "How is it going with your grandmother?" he inquired. "She's so excited to see you. You are the one she always talks about. Don't be too hard on her. You know, she's getting very old. She's been through a lot and now she just needs to take it easy. You know she never leaves her apartment. Nurten goes to see her once a week, but she's all alone. She won't come here to Bursa very often." Looking at me closely, my uncle said, "I can't believe how much you look like your mother. Her death hit us all very hard. She was just so young, and we never expected it. Then, to have you taken to Canada like that, it was like reliving the loss all over again."

"I know that, Uncle," I implored, "It's just that she's so critical and has an opinion for everything. I feel smothered. I just don't know how to talk to her. When she wants to watch serious shows on TV all the time, I want to watch trashy music videos, and when I want to talk about serious issues, she wants to talk about clothes."

"Appearances are serious for her," my uncle responded. "She spent her whole life keeping the family together. Don't take it lightly."

"It's true," one of my cousins chimed in, "Grandma is a fe-min-ist. She can understand three languages and take care of the entire family! Were you seriously watching pop-music videos at her place? She must have been going out of her mind!"

"I can't believe that a person could strikingly resemble another person like this! It's absolutely incredible!" my uncle uttered in disbelief, staring at me as though he were seeing a ghost. "Be kind to her. She's been through a lot, but she's always been very critical of the ones she loves the most. You know, you're a lot like your mother, and she was always stubborn. As a matter of fact, she never liked being told what to do, either."

It was difficult to remember my uncle's words as I was preparing to return to my life in Canada. My grandmother and I were both anxious and sad to say goodbye once again.

"Listen, why don't you let your cousin come with you into Sultan Ahmet? There are a lot of dangerous foreigners at the market. You have to be careful with those people. Why don't you dress properly? You're not eating well, you know. You only had two pieces of toast and half a cup of tea today. You've been travelling five weeks and spent only two of them in Istanbul. I made you three new outfits while you were here and you haven't worn any of them more than once," she said, summing up my visit in a matter of seconds. "I don't understand why you're so difficult. Have you been to the doctor? Your nerves are a mess! There are drugs they can give you for these sort of things, you know. Oh, and your shirt needs ironing. Don't you dare go out before I iron it!"

"Mother!" I said, feeling as though I wanted to jump right out of the open window and into the cushiony clouds. "I love you."

"I know you do," she replied, as she gazed over my shoulder to the large picture of the woman no one talked about. "Don't forget to write and call once in a while when you get back to Canada. Don't wait too long before you come back to visit again, understand? I'm turning 75 this year," she said. "Remember that."

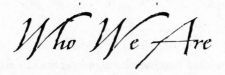
Who We Are

CHRISTINE BELLINI

Christine is a psychotherapist in private practice in Toronto. She is a graduate of York University and is active in both the feminist and Italian communities. She gives special thanks to *la familia* for years of food, conversation, laughter and support.

JO-ANNE BERMAN

Jo-Anne is a freelance writer and editor. Her grandmother is with her every day, symbolized in the wedding band, once her grandmother's, that Jo-Anne wears every day.

ALANNA F. BONDAR

Alanna, a Sault Ste. Marie native, is currently pursuing her Ph.D. in English literature at Memorial University in Newfoundland. Her concern for ecological and feminist issues informs much of her creative and academic work. "Seeing through Amber-Coloured Glasses" arose from her desire to discover more about her personal and cultural roots. Alanna resides in Stratford, Ontario, where she writes for fringe theatre and plans to complete her first novel by the turn of the century.

KAREN DIAZ

Karen enjoys having quiet dinners with her husband, Kevin, and attending her two sons' rambunctious hockey games. She is looking forward to Kevin completing the West Indian cookbook on which he is working. It was a promise he made to Mama a long time ago. Apparently, no one can make "stew chicken" like Mama, so Karen and her sisters have a vested interest in ensuring that the cookbook does justice to Mama's attentiveness to culinary details.

HARRIETT GRANT

Harriett is currently trying to live by her grandmother's creed: "Do all that you can now that you're young, because when you're older you may not be able to do it." This creed has inspired Harriett to fulfil her childhood dream of touring Europe. She has recently accomplished another important goal by writing this story about her grandmother. Harriett hopes to continue to seize the day as it unfolds before her.

VIVIAN HANSEN

Vivian lives with her very Canadian teenage daughter in Calgary. She writes, as her mother and grandmother did, breathing life into stories and the collective work of women.

NATSUKO KOKUBU

Natsuko is presently studying bio-psychology at Concordia University. She aspires to be a veterinarian one day. The animal kingdom fascinates Natsuko, for she loves the innocence of animals and believes that they instinctively know their place in the universe. Initially Natsuko wrote the short tales for her story in Japanese, as a way to connect more intimately with her grandmother.

ANNA LUSTERIO

Anna, Nora's older sister, is an aspiring stonemason with a B.A. in Sociology from McGill University. She lives in Montreal with her husband Perry and their two children and has worked as a journalist, tabloid editor and freelance desktop publisher. "Passages" is the two sisters' first creative collaborative effort, unless you count the deck railing they built together in 1996.

NORA LUSTERIO

Nora has an M.A. in Literature from the University of British Columbia but secretly aspires to become a carpenter. In the meantime, she vents her creative energy as a speech writer. Nanay was the mainstay of Nora's childhood, and her spirit continues to be a profound and influential force in her life.

NICOLA LYLE

Born in Belfast, Northern Ireland, Nicola currently resides in Toronto with her beloved, Adam. The recent birth of their baby girl, Maya Elizabeth, continues the enduring tradition of her grandmother's name, legacy and spirit. Nicola is currently combining full-time motherhood with graduate studies in community development at the University of Toronto.

HELEN (BAJOREK) MACDONALD

Helen is in the final stretch of her M.A. at Trent University. Her thesis topic is Polish survivors of Second World War Siberian labour camps who made Canada their home after the war. "Grand[M]Other Tongue" was inspired by her babcia, who never discussed the experience. Helen is past editor of AVANCER: *The Student Journal for the Study of Canada*. Her writing has been published in a number of Canadian newspapers, magazines and academic journals.

ELPIDA MORFETAS

Elpida was born in Athens, Greece, and raised in Toronto after immigrating with her grandmother in 1971. In addition to the many stories her yiayia left behind, she possesses an extensive collection of cheap religious trinkets, which are priceless. Elpida is currently teaching English and hopes to carry on her yiayia's storytelling traditions. She will one day visit Syros and sunbathe on the rocks.

ALYS MURPHY

Alys's daughter, very much her own woman, is for Alys a visible expression of the strength, beauty and integrity of all the women in her family, and she is Alys's greatest joy. Other joys of her life are green growing things, fiery sunsets, prairie winds and tumbling waters. Alys's will to wage a daily struggle against oppression and violence against women is sustained by energy drawn from these joys and sorrows. Writing this story put closure on decades of shame, grief and bitterness that were the residue of Alys's experience as a Ukrainian child torn between loyalty to a warm, loving family and pleasing an outside world that clearly disliked them.

DIMPLE RAJA

In grade eight Dimple's history teacher brought in an archaeologist, who had recently returned from an Inca expedition in Peru, to talk to the class. Since that day Dimple has been intrigued by diverse cultures and history. She is fascinated by how cultures were formed – what they were rather than what they are today. Exploring the past provides more insight than we care to admit at times.

SUSAN EVANS SHAW

Susan was born in North Bay, Ontario, a location unplanned by her mother, who was unexpectedly displaced from the Sudbury hospital at the end of the Second World War. Chance and change have played an important role in Susan's life ever since. Most recently, a series of unforeseen events allowed her to realize a childhood dream of becoming a writer. Susan lives at the top of a high-rise in Hamilton with her geologist husband and their two cats.

EVA TIHANYI

Eva has one husband, one son, two cats and a number of close friends who encourage her penchant for wine-soaked conversation. She spends as much time as she can in her study (located in Welland, Ontario), where she daydreams of hedonistic pursuits to be financed by the writing, teaching, reviewing and editing she does in her spare time. Her fourth poetry collection, *Restoring the Wickedness,* is forthcoming from Thistledown Press in 2000. Eva's favourite fruit is the apple, into which she bites shamelessly.

GINA VALLE

At least once a day Gina asks herself what this journey on earth is all about, and why we spend so much time running and so little time connecting. The moments Gina cherishes the most are those spent with family and friends over a meal or caffè latte. This creative collection of stories is a tribute to her grandmother, who turned 94 as it went to press.

ZEYNEP VAROGLU

Zeynep enjoys drinking tea and reading the newspaper in cafés just before sunset.

ERIKA WILLAERT

Erika is a second-generation Chinese Canadian. Born in Toronto, she now lives in Aurora, Ontario, with her husband, Karel, and their two cats, Kasper and Hobbes. She teaches grade seven in Richmond Hill and enjoys dance, travel and working with kids. This is her first publication of prose.

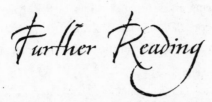

Further Reading

Andersen, Margret, comp. *Mother Was Not a Person.* Montreal: Black Rose Books, 1974.

Bissoondath, Neil. *Selling Illusions: The Cult of Multiculturalism in Canada.* Toronto: Penguin Books, 1994.

Boynton, Marilyn Irwin, and Mary Dell. *Goodbye Mother, Hello Woman: Reweaving the Daughter-Mother Relationship.* Toronto: Daughter-Mother Press, 1994.

Brown, Loranne. *The Handless Maiden.* Toronto: Doubleday, 1998.

Buss, Helen M. *Mapping Our Selves: Canadian Women's Autobiography in English.* Montreal: McGill-Queen's University Press, 1993.

——. *Memoirs from Away: A New Found Land Girlhood.* Waterloo: Wilfred Laurier University Press, 1999.

Chang, Jung. *Wild Swans: Three Daughters of China.* New York: Anchor-Doubleday, 1992.

Charon, Milly, ed. *Between Two Worlds: The Canadian Immigrant Experience.* Montreal: Nu-age Editions, 1988.

Chong, Denise. *The Concubine's Children.* Toronto: Penguin Books, 1995.

Conway, Jill Ker. *When Memory Speaks: Reflections on Autobiography.* New York: Knopf, 1998.

Cook, Mariana. *Generations of Women: In Their Own Words.* San Francisco: Chronicle Books, 1998.

Giovanni, Nikki. *Grandparents: Poems, Reminiscences and Short Stories About the Keepers of Our Tradition.* New York: Henry Holt, 1994.

Haas, Maara. *The Street Where I Live.* Toronto: McGraw-Hill Ryerson, 1976.

Harris, Claire. *Drawing Down a Daughter.* Fredericton: Goose Lane Editions, 1992.

Heffron, Dorris. *A Shark in the House.* Toronto: Key Porter Books, 1996.

Heilbrun, Carolyn G. *Writing a Woman's Life.* New York: Ballantine Books, 1988.

Hutcheon, Linda, and Marion Richmond, eds. *Other Solitudes: Canadian Multicultural Fictions.* Toronto: Oxford University Press, 1990.

Kack-Brice, Valerie, ed. *For She Is the Tree of Life: Grandmothers Through the Eyes of Women Writers.* Berkeley: Conari Press, 1995.

Karpinski, Eva C., ed. *Pens of Many Colours: A Canadian Reader*. Toronto: Harcourt Brace Jovanovich, 1993.

Knowles, Valerie. *Strangers at Our Gates: Canadian Immigration and Immigration Policy, 1540-1997*. Rev. ed. Toronto: Dundurn Press, 1997.

Kogawa, Joy. *Itsuka*. Toronto: Penguin Books, 1992.

——. *Obasan*. Toronto: Penguin Books, 1981.

Kostash, Myrna. *All of Baba's Children*. Edmonton: Hurtig, 1977.

Kulyk Keefer, Janice. *Honey and Ashes: A Story of Family*. Toronto: Harper-Flamingo, 1998.

Lee, Sky. *Disappearing Moon Cafe*. Vancouver: Douglas and McIntyre, 1990.

Manguel, Alberto, ed. *Mothers & Daughters: An Anthology*. Vancouver: Raincoast Books, 1998.

Martz, Sandra, and Shirley Coe, eds. *Generation to Generation: Reflections on Friendships Between Young and Old*. Watsonville, CA: Papier-Mache Press, 1998.

Moss, Lisa Braver. *Celebrating Family: Our Lifelong Bonds with Parents and Siblings*. Berkeley: Wildcat Canyon Press-Circulus Publishing Group, 1998.

Mukherjee, Arun. *Postcolonialism: My Living*. Toronto: Tsar, 1998.

——, ed. *Sharing Our Experience*. Ottawa: Canadian Advisory Council on the Status of Women, 1993.

Reddy, Maureen T., Martha Roth, and Amy Sheldon, eds. *Mother Journeys: Feminists Write About Mothering*. Minneapolis: Spinsters Ink, 1994.

Shapiro, Judith, comp. *The Source of the Spring: Mothers Through the Eyes of Women Writers*. Berkeley: Conari Press, 1998.

Silvera, Makeda, ed. *The Other Women: Women of Colour in Contemporary Canadian Literature*. Toronto: Sister Vision Press, 1995.

Tan, Amy. *The Joy Luck Club*. New York: Putnam's, 1989.

Wassermann, Selma. *The Long Distance Grandmother: How to Stay Close to Distant Grandchildren*. 3rd ed. Vancouver: Hartley and Marks, 1996.

Wiebe, Katie Funk. *The Storekeeper's Daughter: A Canadian Reader*. Waterloo: Herald Press, 1997.

Wylie, Betty Jane. *Reading Between the Lines: The Diaries of Women*. Toronto: Key Porter Books, 1995.

Zweig, Connie, ed. *To Be a Woman: The Birth of the Conscious Feminine*. Los Angeles: Jeremy Tarcher, 1990.

Acknowledgements

The completion of this collection is a special achievement for me. Working on *Our Grandmothers, Ourselves: Reflections of Canadian Women* has brought me great challenges and immeasurable joy. I have come to learn that with vision, hard work and patience, dreams can come true. I am particularly indebted to my parents, Domenico and Giuseppina Valle, and my grandmother, Luigina Valle, whose quiet presence and unconditional love continues to give me strength no matter where I find myself in the world.

I am grateful to those who have helped make this book possible. Many thanks go to Dr. Grace Feuerverger, for gently encouraging me to ask difficult questions and to find my voice; to Dr. Michael Connelly, whose belief in the power of narrative has shaped my personal and professional work; to Anna Panunto, who worked as tirelessly on this project as if it were her own, and without whose support it could not have been completed; to Alberto Di Giovanni, for believing in this multicultural collection; to Andrée Paquette and Kala Limbani, for generously giving of their time in preparing the manuscript as it progressed through its various stages; to the contributors, whose patience and vision were of paramount importance; to Ivana Barbieri, for her collegiality and spirit of generosity; to Marie Louise Donald, for her legal input and her *joie de vivre*; to Tom Boreskie, Lucy Niro and JoAnn Phillion, for their editorial support; and to the Canada Council for the Arts and the Multiculturalism Program of Canadian Heritage for their assistance.

My fondest thanks are due to David Chemla, my companion and husband, who has given me endless support and encouragement over the years. With his gentle advice, wealth of editorial expertise and warm sense of humour, all obstacles in life seem surmountable. His compassion and insightful suggestions guide me in all aspects of my work. Thank you, David, for the gifts you give me each day.